An Islamic Jihad of Nonviolence

An Islamic Jihad of Nonviolence

SAID NURSI'S MODEL

Salih Sayilgan

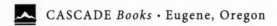

 CASCADE *Books* · Eugene, Oregon

AN ISLAMIC JIHAD OF NONVIOLENCE
Said Nursi's Model

Cascade Books
An Imprint of Wipf and Stock Publishers
199 W. 8th Ave., Suite 3
Eugene, OR 97401

www.wipfandstock.com

PAPERBACK ISBN: 978-1-5326-5755-9
HARDCOVER ISBN: 978-1-5326-5756-6
EBOOK ISBN: 978-1-5326-5757-3

Cataloguing-in-Publication data:

Names: Sayilgan, Salih.
Title: AN ISLAMIC JIHAD OF NONVIOLENCE : Said Nursi's model / Salih Sayilgan.
Description: Eugene, OR: Cascade Books, 2019 | Includes bibliographical references.
Identifiers: ISBN 978-1-5326-5755-9 (paperback) | ISBN 978-1-5326-5756-6 (hardcover) | ISBN 978-1-5326-5757-3 (ebook)
Subjects: LCSH: Jihad | Jihad—History | Nursi, Said—1873–1960 | Nonviolence—Religious aspects—Islam | Islam—Doctrines | War (Islamic law)
Classification: BP182 S19 2019 (print) | BP182 (ebook)

Manufactured in the U.S.A.   DECEMBER 4, 2018

Dedicated to the students of the *Risale-i Nur* for their peaceful *jihad*.

We are competitors of love; we have no time for enmity.

—BEDIÜZZAMAN SAID NURSI

Table of Contents

Acknowledgements

WORDS WILL REMAIN INSUFFICIENT to express my gratitude for the support I received while working on this project. I would like to begin by acknowledging the work of Şükran Vahide, who has been a pioneering scholar in Nursi studies. This project relies significantly on her translation of the *Risale-i Nur*, as well as her biographical work on Said Nursi.

I am grateful to Lucinda Mosher for editing the first draft of the manuscript and making valuable suggestions. Special thanks go to Ahmet Yıldız, Alparslan Açıkgenç, and Faris Kaya who read and provided important ideas for improving the manuscript. I am also grateful to Niyazi Beki and Hakan Gülerce for helping me with the research while working on this project. The editorial team of Cascade made the publication of this work a smooth process. I am especially thankful to Matthew Wimer, Daniel Lanning, Heather Carraher, my editor Robin Parry, and my copyeditor, Caleb Shupe.

My deepest appreciation goes to my wife Zeyneb and daughter Elif. Zeyneb not only read the manuscript and made significant suggestions for improvement, but also provided love and care. Without her support, I could not have concluded this project.

Introduction

IT IS NOT UNCOMMON to see Islam and Muslims mentioned alongside terrorism and violence. Let alone popular media, one can even observe these names side by side in the title of courses offered at universities.

In mainstream media and among the general public, three misleading assertions concerning Islam seem to be constantly at play. First is the assertion that Islam is inherently a violent religion. Selected verses from the Qur'an and some of the traditional sayings of the Prophet Muhammad are routinely cited as evidence, along with noting that the Prophet himself was involved in many battles and that wars were a factor in the expansion of the Muslim state and the establishment of the Islamic empire. Thus it is argued that Islam was spread through *jihad* and sword. But, to bolster this assertion further, its proponents point to violence committed in the name of Islam and conflict rampant in certain Muslim societies today.

A second assertion is that Islam is a political ideology rather than a source of meaning, values, and spirituality for its adherents. This is founded in part on the fact that, during the twentieth century, many Muslims did believe that political Islam could solve the problems of Muslim societies. The idea was that an Islamic government would serve best in ruling a society based on Islamic values.

A third assertion is that Islam is unable to accommodate a secular environment that is tolerant to religion. That is, in order to live a life in accordance with God's will, one must live in a society that is ruled according to Islamic law (*sharia*)—a notion many Muslims do, in fact, believe.

The thesis of this book is that there exists an Islamic model that offers a direct challenge to these three assertions, a model provided by the distinguished Muslim theologian Bediuzzaman Said Nursi (1877–1960). A charismatic and deeply spiritual personality who witnessed the collapse of the Ottoman Empire and the emergence of modern Turkey, Nursi was determined to offer new resources to bridge the gap caused by the establishment of a new secular state that terminated the institutions providing religious education and nurturing Islamic spirituality. This became his daily *jihad*, the price for which he would be exiled and imprisoned. This book relates the history and method of spiritual *jihad*—with positive action (*müsbet hareket*) as its hallmark—as taught and demonstrated by Bediuzzaman Said Nursi. It lays out the guidelines he provided to aid Muslims in living a peaceful and spiritual life in a secular environment.

Chapter 1 situates Nursi in his historical context. Chapter 2 provides a brief overview of his *magnum opus*, the *Risale-i Nur*, examining its emergence and its major themes. Chapter 3 is a survey of the notions of *jihad* and martyrdom in Islam. Chapter 4 presents the foundations of Nursi's philosophy of positive action (*müsbet hareket*) as well as his view of suffering and death. Chapter 5 defines the components of inward *jihad* in Nursi's writings: impotence (*acz*), poverty (*fakr*), compassion (*şefkat*), and contemplation (*tefekkür*)—and the steps for cultivating them. Chapter 6 provides Nursi's interpretation of *jihad* and martyrdom in the modern time and his view of other faiths. Chapter 7 presents Nursi's guidelines for the community of believers in the modern context: his emphasis on sincerity (*ihlas*), free service to faith (*iman*), avoidance of politics, rejection of hierarchy, and the preference of community over and against excessive individualism.

In chapter 8, Nursi is put in conversation with three of his contemporaries—major figures with a profound commitment to non-violent forms of civil disobedience: Mohandas Gandhi (1869–1948), Nelson Mandela (1918–2013), and Martin Luther King Jr. (1929–68). Each risked his life in the pursuit of justice. Each was imprisoned because of the position he took. Each was a charismatic figure whose teachings and example enabled a dramatic transformation of their respective societies. As will be demonstrated, Nursi belongs into their company.

This work concludes with a consideration of the usefulness of Nursi's model of positive action (*müsbet hareket*) emphasizing spiritual or moral *jihad* (*cihad-ı mānevī*) and examines it as a method for facing the challenges of the twenty-first century.

PART 1

Said Nursi

Chapter 1

Said Nursi's Life and Context

The Formation of Nursi

Bediuzzaman Said Nursi (1877–1960 CE) was a Muslim child prodigy, scholar, spiritual leader, and educational reformer. His literary legacy, the *Risale-i Nur*—a six-thousand-page commentary on the Qur'an—has made an ongoing claim on an extensive and rapidly expanding group of people in Turkey and beyond.

In his lifetime, Nursi saw the dissolution of the Ottoman Empire, endured the anti-Islamic policies of Turkey's post-World War I Republican People's Party, and enjoyed the somewhat improved conditions established by Turkey's democratic government. He is best described as an Islamic revivalist. A brief explanation of Nursi's historical context will give us a better understanding of the roots of his positive action (*müsbet hareket*) and ethic of nonviolence.

Referring to the century before Nursi was born, Marshal Hodgson, the renowned historian of Islam, describes the situation of the Muslim world in this way: "Though the eighteenth century was not without its interesting and creative figures, it was probably the least notable of all in achievement of high-cultural excellence; the relative barrenness was practically universal in Muslim lands."[1] The Muslim world was in physical and psychological decline in almost all aspects: militarily, culturally, economically, and socially. Although, in the eighteenth century, the portion of Muslim

1. Hodgson, *Venture of Islam*, 134.

3

lands occupied by the European powers was small, the dominant presence of the West was felt everywhere in the Muslim world. By the turn of the nineteenth century, the Western powers—along with the Russians—were overwhelmingly dominating most of the rest of the world, in particular the Muslim territories.[2] Typically, notes Hodgson, even if there would be no direct colonization of a Muslim power, "in any case, no independent general Islamic leadership was to be tolerated."[3]

The situation of the Muslim world in the early twentieth century was even more dramatic. Almost the entire Muslim world was controlled by the European powers. While the British colonized Egypt, Palestine, Iraq, and India, the French controlled North Africa and Syria. The European hegemony even included Dutch control of Indonesia and Malaysia, with the British eventually taking control of the latter.[4] As rightly put by Tamara Sonn, "from this vantage point, it began to look like the Crusades were on again."[5]

The state of the Ottoman territories was not much different. The situation of the Ottomans was as dramatic as in other parts of the Muslim world. With the military defeats and decline, the Ottomans were also in a desperate position. As a response, the rulers attempted to initiate reforms starting with the military. The questions facing the empire were not only about the economic decline. The Christians of the Balkans—another population of the empire—were inflamed with nationalistic feelings. They were seeking all kinds of means to dismember the empire and to become independent states.[6]

The Ottoman authorities were seeking reforms in order to maintain the state's independence and acquire the military strength of the Europeans.[7] They partly modernized the forces of the army. Schools teaching modern knowledge were set up. Some of the Western dress styles were introduced, including the wearing of the fez.[8] In the end, the reforms did not save the Ottomans from stagnation. They failed to meet the purposes.

2. Hodgson, *Venture of Islam*, 177.

3. Hodgson, *Venture of Islam*, 223.

4. Sonn, *Islam: A Brief History*, 114–15.

5. Sonn, *Islam: A Brief History*, 114.

6. Hodgson, *Venture of Islam*, 228.

7. Hodgson, *Venture of Islam*, 231.

8. Hodgson, *Venture of Islam*, 229.

Saving the Empire:
Ottoman Intellectuals Seeking Solutions

Within this context, Ottoman intellectuals were also seeking solutions to the problem. Among them was Said Nursi. He was born in 1877 in Nurs, a village in the province of Bitlis in the eastern part of the Ottoman Empire, during the first year of the First Constitutional Era (*Birinci Meşrutiyet Devri*).[9] Also known as the constitutional monarchy period, the first Western-style parliament under the Ottoman rule was established during this time. Leading figures aimed to protect the empire from collapsing by imposing regulations. The First Constitution intended to establish freedom of religion and equality of all citizens before the law. The effort was short-lived. This era lasted only until the beginning of 1878.

As Ibrahim Abu-Rabi' rightly highlights, nineteenth-century intellectual reactions to the "question of modernity and the threat it posed to the integrity of the Ottoman state" took several forms.[10] The first one was a nationalist response aimed to unite all the Turks under one umbrella. This response was represented by Turkish nationalists. They aimed to unite all the Turks in order to have one language, one ethnicity, and a shared tradition under the empire. The most prominent among them were Ziya Gökalp, Yusuf Akcura, Ahmed Agayev (later Ağaoğlu), and Halim Sabit.[11] The nationalists initiated a new understanding of Turkish civilization that emphasized pre-Islamic Turkish history. An account of Turkish history would no longer begin with the conversion of the Turks to Islam. The nationalists focused very much on a "purification" of the Turkish language to eliminate the influence of Arabic and Persian vocabulary. They even attempted to remove Arabic and Persian elements in Turkish literary works in order to create a national literature. In addition, the nationalists diverted their attention to pre-Islamic Turkish and French literature.

The second reaction aimed to preserve the Ottoman Empire "without giving any central role to Islam in either society or politics."[12] The representatives of this response are called the Westernists. For them, the only way to save the empire was through a process of westernization. In their

9. There is no agreement on the date of Nursi's birth. In most of the sources, the date given for his birth is either 1876 or 1877.

10. Abu-Rabi', *Spiritual Dimensions*, vii.

11. Berkes, *Development of Secularism in Turkey*, 345.

12. Abu-Rabi', *Spiritual Dimensions*, vii.

eyes, "a radical moral and mental transformation" was necessary in order to "develop a new morality based upon the Western system of values."[13] Tevfik Fikret (d. 1915) and Abdullah Cevdet (d. 1932) were among the prominent figures of this school.

The latter, Abdullah Cevdet, believed that the source of the troubles in the empire and later on in modern Turkey was not the ruler *per se*. What had to be changed was society itself. The masses had to be enlightened; otherwise, the whole process of revolution would fail.[14] Cevdet began to publish a review called *Içtihad* while in exile in Geneva. For him, remedies for the empire were obvious and simple: "to push, pull, if necessary lash the people into moving, working, earning, seeing, and thinking like the infidels of the West."[15] Civilization meant, for Cevdet, European culture.[16] In his writings, he initiated an open campaign against Islamic culture. Cevdet first started by translating the works of some of the orientalists on Islam into Turkish. Among them was Reinhart Dozy's (d. 1883) controversial work entitled *De Voornaamste Godsdiensten: Het Islamisme* or *The Main Religions: Islamism*. The translation of Dozy's study was a critical point in Ottoman history, as it was the first time that a book explicitly hostile to Islam and its Prophet had been published in Turkish and widely distributed.[17]

Later on, Cevdet made other attempts to transform Turkish society. He would not hesitate to question the basic tenets of Islam. The April 1927 edition of the monthly magazine *Resimli Ay Mecmuası*, for instance, carried an interview of a number of well-known figures—Abdullah Cevdet among them. As reported there, when asked whether he believed in the Hereafter, Cevdet answered emphatically in the negative, stating that belief in God is only for simpletons and the "irremediably illogical."[18] Further, he asserted that Islam is violent—the religion of blood and war.[19] Later, in the publication *Içtihad*, Cevdet proposed the Bahá'í faith as a replacement for Islam in Turkish society.[20] Over time, the ideology of Westernists like him would greatly influence the direction of modern Turkey.

13. Berkes, *Development of Secularism in Turkey* 338.

14. Berkes, *Development of Secularism in Turkey*, 339.

15. Berkes, *Development of Secularism in Turkey*, 341.

16. Lewis, *Emergence of Modern Turkey*, 267.

17. Hanioğlu, "Garbcılar," 138.

18. Şahiner, *Haşir Risalesi Nasıl Yazıldı*, 31–32.

19. Demir, *Cumhuriyet Aydınlarının İslam'a Bakışı*, 253.

20. Cevdet, "Mezheb-i Bahaullah," 3015–17.

The third response to save the empire, called the Islamist approach, was to some extent a reaction to the Westernist school. The Islamists aimed to modernize the empire while "preserving the status of Islam in that society."[21] Their ideology was initially advanced by the Tanzimatists—intellectuals who believed that the problems that the empire faced could be solved through reforms in institutions related to education, the economy, and the military. They held the view that, under the sultan's sovereignty, all ethnic groups and religious communities were citizens of the Ottoman state with equal political rights.[22] For a while, this position was supported by the Young Ottomans and aimed to unite all nations of the empire under a powerful central government, regardless of their ethnic and religious differences. Islamism, which generally went hand in hand with support for the constitutional regime, found initial support among prominent figures like Mustafa Sabri, Mehmet Akif, Said Halim Paşa, Eşref Edip, Selahaddin Asım, İskilipli Mehmet Atıf, Babanzade A. Naim, A. Hamdi Akseki, and Ismail Hakkı. They all proposed solutions for the problems of the empire.

By contrast, the Islamists used all their efforts to fight against the conviction that Islam was an obstacle to progress. When the Westernists raised their voices to question the religion of Islam regarding some controversial issues, the Islamists were quick to oppose them. Mustafa Sabri, a leading figure of the Islamists, wrote a series of articles entitled "The Controversial Questions of the Religion of Islam" in *Beyan al-Hak* (the "Herald of Truth"). In his articles, Mustafa Sabri addressed contentious issues such as polygamy, divorce, and the permissibility of being photographed.[23] Mehmet Akif, another prominent figure among the Islamists who is also the author of the Turkish National Anthem, promoted the ideology of the school through his poems. Combating a disillusioned westernization and nationalism was the major objective of poems such as his *How Was Your Mind Occupied With the Sentiment of Division?*:

> While Islam should have tightly united you
> I do not understand and cannot understand,
>
> How was your mind occupied with the sentiment of division?
> Did Satan put the idea of nationalism in your mind?

21. Abu-Rabiʿ, *Spiritual Dimensions*, vii.
22. Vahide, *Islam in Modern Turkey*, 58.
23. Berkes, *Development of Secularism in Turkey*, 340.

It was Islam holding under one religion,
Many nations, which were totally different from each other

Nationalism is like an earthquake that destroys from the bottom
If you do not understand this, it is a great disappointment . . .

This nation does not remain standing by emphasizing Albanian and Arab,
The latest policy is Turkish nationalism, which will not work either . . .

God created you all as a family,
Remove all the elements that cause division among you . . .[24]

Here, Akif stresses, only Islam can hold all the nations within the empire.
For him, there is no nationalism in Islam at all. In another poem, Akif criticizes those who see Islam as an obstacle to progress:

Particularly during the declaration of this damned war,
Spit on the faces of those who suggest the absurdity of
"The only way to think like the Westerners is
To leave God out of life" as faith to the people![25]

As is evident, Akif criticizes those who argue that the solution to save the Empire is in blindly following the West and giving up the religion of Islam.[26]

The Old Said: Seeking Solutions in Politics

On any list of prominent figures supporting Islamic values in early twentieth-century Turkey, the name of Said Nursi must be included. Like other members of the Islamist school of thought, Nursi believed that there was an immediate need for change in order to save the empire. He nevertheless maintained that change should be based on the principles of the religion of Islam. In the first phase of his life—that is, his life as the Old Said—Nursi had dedicated his energy to that cause. He had completed his education at various traditional schools (*medrese*) in the eastern part of the empire and contemplated its problems by analyzing the eastern provinces.

24. Ersoy, *Safahat*, 163–64. The translation was made by the author.

25. Ersoy, *Safahat*, 186. The translation was made by the author.

26. This part is a revised version of a section from one of my articles. For more details see Sayilgan, "Importance of the *Sunna*," 192–94.

Given his location in the eastern province of the Ottoman Empire during most of the first decades of his life, one might wonder how Nursi became aware of the problems in the Ottoman lands and the Muslim world in general. There are several answers to this. First, Nursi did not remain in one location during his formative years. Before making his first visit to Istanbul in 1907, Nursi had already visited many places in Eastern Anatolia and studied in different Islamic schools (*medrese*). Second, during his time in Mardin, a city in the southeast of Turkey, Nursi met a student of Jamal al-Din al-Afghani (d. 1897) and a member of the religious Sanusi Sufi order.[27] Al-Afghani was an influential figure of Islamic modernism seeking solutions for the questions of the Muslim world. He was an advocate of pan-Islamism. In addition, the Sanusi Sufi order was a prominent revivalist movement that emerged in Libya and the central Sahara in the early 1840s. The order is known for its resistance against the French and Italian colonialist powers. Nursi's encounter with these two men likely had an impact on his political awareness, as well as his knowledge concerning the state of the Muslim world.[28]

Third, while in Van, a city in the eastern part of Turkey, Nursi stayed at the residence of the governor Tahir Pasha for a long period. Tahir Pasha supported Nursi until his death in 1913. This period is exceptionally significant in Nursi's life. Tahir Pasha was an esteemed bureaucrat of Sultan Abdulhamid II and a well-known supporter of education. He had a wide-ranging library and followed developments in the West and modern science with great interest. The governor's residence was a preferred meeting place for other government officials, teachers, and other intellectuals in order to discuss various questions of interest.[29]

According to Turner, it was probably while staying at the governor's residence that Nursi concluded that a new interpretation of Islamic theology was essential: "Nursi realized for the first time that traditional Muslim theology alone was unable to answer the doubts concerning Islam that had been raised as a result of the growth of materialism, and that a study of modern science was necessary."[30] While there, Nursi took full advantage of

27. Turner and Horkuc, *Makers of Islamic Civilization*, 10. See also Vahide, *Islam in Modern Turkey*, 22–23.

28. Unfortunately, there is no documentation available regarding the exact content and exchange they had.

29. Vahide, *Islam in Modern Turkey*, 27.

30. Turner and Horkuc, *Makers of Islamic Civilization*, 11.

Tahir Pasha's library and the newspapers and journals delivered to him. He studied a wide range of books on social and natural sciences—including history, geography, mathematics, geology, physics, chemistry, astronomy, and philosophy. Nursi was therefore able to gain insight into the broader problems challenging Ottoman society and the wider Muslim world.[31]

Having become increasingly aware of the problems affecting Muslim communities around the globe, Nursi began to develop solutions—starting with the promotion of educational reforms. In founding his own *madrasa* or Islamic seminary in Van, Nursi formulated and implemented new ideas in order to advocate reforms in education. He aimed to combine the religious sciences with modern sciences. For him, this combination would corroborate and strengthen the truths of religion. Nursi practiced this new method when he was teaching his own students.[32] Later on, he took his new method of education further and wanted to establish a university that would embody his ideas in Eastern Anatolia. He named the university the *Medresetü'z-Zehra* after the Al-Azhar University in Cairo, as it was to be its sister university in the center of the western Islamic world.[33] Nursi's hope was that the new project would be a significant means of combating the widespread ignorance and backwardness of the region and also finding solutions for its social and political problems.

During his time with the government officials in Van, Nursi grew quite alarmed at the extent of Westernization and secularization at the degree to which doubts about Islam were expressed among the Ottoman elite. Some of these officials had concluded that Islam was responsible for the backwardness of the Ottoman state. Nursi knew that an urgent reform in education was necessary and "the updating of the Islamic sciences in the light of modern advances in knowledge" was a requisite.[34] This thought occupied Nursi's mind until the beginning of World War I.

With his project in mind, Nursi left Van for Istanbul in 1907 to realize his dreams of reforming the Islamic educational system. A reference letter written by Tahir Pasha helped Nursi to meet the Sultan. Nursi nevertheless received no support for his project on this occasion, but he had the opportunity to meet some members of the Young Turks who were the leading

31. Vahide, *Islam in Modern Turkey*, 36.
32. Vahide, *Islam in Modern Turkey*, 29.
33. Vahide, *Islam in Modern Turkey*, 29.
34. Vahide, *Islam in Modern Turkey*, 29.

figures of the reformation movement in the empire.[35] The Young Turks discovered Nursi's vision and were aware of his influence on society. Later on, Nursi became involved in their activities. Three days after the Young Turks' success against Sultan Abdulhamid II in 1908, Nursi delivered a speech entitled "Address to Freedom" at an event organized by the Young Turks' Committee of Union and Progress in Istanbul, repeating it later in Salonica's Freedom Square. In it, he said:

> O Freedom! . . . I convey these glad tidings to you, that if you make the *Shari'ah*, which is life itself, the source of life, and if you grow in that paradise, this oppressed nation will progress a thousand times further than in former times. If, that is, it takes you as its guide in all matters and does not besmirch you through harboring personal enmity and thoughts of revenge . . . Freedom has exhumed us from the grave of desolation and despotism, and summoned us to the paradise of unity and love of nation.
>
> The doors of a suffering-free paradise of progress and civilization have been opened to us . . . The constitution, which is in accordance with the *Shari' ah*, is the introduction to the sovereignty of the nation and invites us to enter like the treasury-guard of paradise. O my oppressed compatriots! Let us go and enter![36]

As evident, Nursi argues that taking the side of constitutionalism is a religious obligation because of the emphasis on the concept of *shūrā* or consultation in Islam. Furthermore, he indicates that as long as the constitution is consistent with the principles of Islam, it would be "the means of upholding the might of Islam and exalting the word of God."[37] According to Nursi, material progress was a significant means to uphold the word of God (*ila-yı kelimetullah*) and constitutionalism was one of the ways to achieve this progress. At this stage, Nursi became very involved in political and social life. During the next two years (1908–1910), taking the advantage of new freedom of thought and expression, Nursi delivered speeches, addressed gatherings, and published numerous articles in the newspapers and journals of the day. He was the leading member of several societies, including the Society for Students of the Religious Sciences (*Talebe-i Ulum Cemiyeti*)

35. Mardin, *Religion and Social Change*, 78–79.

36. Nursi, *İlk Dönem Eserleri*, 421–22. Nursi's writings from the Old Said period have not been translated into English yet; however, some passages including this one can be found in Vahide's *Islam in Modern Turkey*, 53–54.

37. Vahide, "Life and Times of Bediuzzaman," 216.

and the Society for Muslim Unity (*Ittihad-ı Muhammedî Cemiyeti*).[38] After the 31 March Incident,[39] however, Nursi was accused of being an instigator and was put on trial by the military court.[40] He was then exonerated. Nursi did not stay long in Istanbul; rather, he set off for Van.[41]

As stated above, Nursi did not dismiss the social reality. At this stage of his life, he was highly active in politics and cooperated with some statesmen and institutions. He initially worked with members of the Young Turks in order to save the empire.[42] From his *Medresetü'z Zehra* project, his articles in various newspapers, and his speeches, one can conclude that Nursi's immediate aim was to save the Ottoman state—that is, he advocated building unity within the empire. Nursi saw education as the most important means to accomplish this unity: "Unity cannot occur through ignorance. Unity is the fusion of ideas, and the fusion of ideas occurs through the electric rays of knowledge."[43] That is, according to Nursi, unity cannot be achieved without education.

During the next two years, in the eastern region of the empire, Nursi travelled to different provinces in order to explain the principles of the freedom movement and constitutionalism at gatherings. Most of the tribes were very concerned that the new reforms and ideas were not consistent with Islamic principles. Yet Nursi passionately advocated constitutionalism. His exchanges with the scholars and tribes were published as *Muhākemāt* (reasonings) and *Münazarāt* (debates).

38. Mardin, *Religion and Social Change*, 84. See also Vahide, *Islam in Modern Turkey*, 66–68, Turner and Horkuc, *Makers of Islamic Civilization*, 15.

39. Known as the 31 March Incident (31 Mart Vakası), the incident broke out in April 1909. It was a revolt against the Young Turks' secular agenda by the traditionalist officers within the Ottoman Army.

40. Mardin, *Religion and Social Change*, 84–85. See also Vahide, *Islam in Modern Turkey*, 76–80.

41. Vahide, *Islam in Modern Turkey*, 83.

42. Although Nursi cooperated with Young Turks in his formative years and supported their Committee of Union and Progress, he later criticized their policies. They also, unlike their first years, dismissed Islamic principles as a base in order to solve the problems of the empire. In a newspaper article that appeared in April of 1909, he replied to the question "In Salonica you cooperated with the Committee of Union and Progress, why did you part from it?" His response was, "I did not part from it; it was some of its members that parted. I am still in agreement with people like Niyazi Bey and Enver Bey, but some of them parted from us. They strayed from the path and headed for the swamp." See Vahide, *Islam in Modern Turkey*, 37.

43. Nursi, "Münazarat," 61, cited in Vahide, *Islam in Modern Turkey*, 37.

In the eastern part, Nursi addressed the concerns of people regarding constitutionalism. They were worried that constitutionalism was incompatible with the *shari'a* or Islamic law. Nursi stated that the essence of constitution and its life were from the *shari'a*. It can certainly be stated that not everything in the constitution is completely suitable to the *shari'a*. However, Nursi remarks, is there anything or any one person that perfectly embodies the *shari'a* in all aspects? Yet, Nursi notes, if 1 percent of the new constitution was inconsistent with the *shari'a*, this would be 100 percent in the case of the old regime's authoritarianism. "We are simply advocating what is better," Nursi says. In addition, Nursi maintained that with the constitution, abuse of power would be less possible than with the previous regime, because it puts forward many obstacles against the exploitation of power.[44]

Alluding to some of the verses in the Qur'an, Nursi stresses that they could be interpreted in favor of constitutionalism. For him, constitutionalism was the manifestation of the qur'anic verses "Consult with them about matters"[45] and "[They] conduct their affairs by mutual consultation."[46] As these verses highlight, consultation among people can be based on the *shari'a*. In line with the teaching of the Qur'an, unlike the previous regime, constitutionalism does not establish itself upon power, but right. "Its heart is education, its language is love, and its mind is law, not a person."[47] Nursi also accentuated that the constitutional government would give everyone an equal status. Every person would rise to the rank of a "sultan," meaning each member of society was equally valuable under the law. That is why everyone should seek to be a sultan by advocating the freedom offered by the constitution.[48]

People also generally raised their concerns about religious minorities. They pointed out that, with the new constitution, there would be a parliament accommodating Jews and Christians and granting them rights. These religious minorities would be part of the process in making the law. Nursi's conversation partners asked him how the vote of Jews and Christians could

44. Nursi, *İlk Dönem Eserleri*, 453.

45. Qur'an 3:159. Unless otherwise indicated, the translations of the verses from the Qur'an are based on M. A. S. Abdel Haleem's translation. See *The Qur'an: English and Parallel Arabic Text.*

46. Qur'an 42:38.

47. Nursi, *İlk Dönem Eserleri*, 443.

48. Nursi, *İlk Dönem Eserleri*, 444.

be considered acceptable and being in accordance with the *shari'a*. In the constitution, Nursi responded, priority would be given to the majority. In addition, a parliamentarian would be free and above any influence. In advocating for a religiously diverse parliament, Nursi pointed to the works of the Armenians and the Jews. In making a watch or machine, he said, it did not matter whether they were made by Armenian Haço or Jewish Berham.[49] What should be at stake is the quality of their works. The *shari'a* is unconcerned about the makers. Likewise, the parliament would mainly deal with the political and economic issues for a better society. Again, the *shari'a* is indifferent as long as the parliament makes laws for the betterment of society. Not to mention that, with the constitutional government, the moral issues and law concerning people's fundamental rights would not be subject to any change. The task of the parliamentarians would be to protect these laws so that Muslim judges (*kadı*) and jurist experts of Islamic law (*müftü*) would not exploit them.[50]

While Nursi persuaded tribal leaders to recognize a constitutional government as advantageous for every member of society, they were still uncomfortable that Greeks and Armenians would be granted the same rights like them. Nursi reassured them by highlighting that non-Muslims' freedom in the context of constitutionalism is not to be subjected to injustice and oppression. This is also the teaching of the *shari'a*.

Nursi further remarked that granting equal rights to the People of the Book (a qur'anic term which refers to Jews and Christians) is part of the law of Islam. A king and a beggar are equal before the law. If a law is concerned even about the protection of an ant, how can it violate the rights of human beings regardless of their religion? Violating people's fundamental rights because of their religion is unlawful according to the *shari'a*.

Nursi then referred to two cases from the history of Islam to support his point. On one occasion, an incident occurred between 'Ali ibn Abi Tālib (d. 661)—the fourth successor after the Prophet Muhammad—and a Jew. Apparently, 'Ali lost his armor and could not locate it. One day, he apparently found it in the possession of the Jewish person. When he asked for the armor, the Jew refused to return it. 'Ali then took the issue to the court. The judge asked him to bring two witnesses to make his case. 'Ali came with his servant and two sons. The judge declined to accept their

49. Nursi symbolically uses common names among Armenians and Jews in the eastern province of the Ottoman Empire.

50. Nursi, *İlk Dönem Eserleri*, 455.

testimony. Because ʿAli did not provide sufficient evidence for the case, the judge decided in favor of the Jewish person.[51] In the other case, Nursi noted an incident between an Armenian Christian and Salahuddin Ayyubi (d. 1193), the founder of the Ayyubid dynasty. Sultan Salahuddin was judged standing next to an Armenian complainant. Addressing the Kurdish tribes, Nursi pointed out that they should at least take the sultan, whom they are so proud of, as an example concerning justice for the People of the Book.[52]

In their conversation with Nursi, people also brought up the hostilities between the Kurds and the Armenians in recent years. Nursi answered that enmity has prevailed due to the authoritarian regime. The solution of a constitutional government would revive a lasting friendship between the two groups. Nursi also stated that the prosperity of the Kurds was rooted in their alliance and friendship with the Armenians. He pointed out that the Kurds needed to extend the hand of peace to them. Enmity is harmful.[53] The Kurds could challenge the Armenians, Nursi indicated, by being awakened like them. They could be confronted with their own weapons, which are reason, nationalism, yearning to progress, and promoting justice. Holding a sword will not benefit. The Kurds needed the sword of reason. In fact, the Armenians could be an inspiration for the Kurds because of their unity, progress, and hard work.[54]

Finally, the leaders asked how they could justify having an Armenian governor for their city, because the constitutional government rendered such an option possible. If people are fine with having an Armenian watchmaker and mechanic, Nursi said, then they should not have an issue with having an Armenian as a governor either. In a constitutional state, people govern. The government officials work for the people. If the right constitution is in place, a governor is not the head of people, but in service of them. This is how Muslim citizens should regard an Armenian governor.[55]

Addressing the Global Muslim Community

From the east, Nursi went further down the south of the empire in the early 1911. This time, his destination was Damascus, which was known as an

51. Nursi, *İlk Dönem Eserleri*, 470.

52. Nursi, *İlk Dönem Eserleri*, 470.

53. Nursi, *İlk Dönem Eserleri*, 470.

54. Nursi, *İlk Dönem Eserleri*, 471.

55. Nursi, *İlk Dönem Eserleri*, 478.

intellectual center of many prominent Muslim scholars. Nursi was asked to deliver a sermon at the famous Umayyad Mosque. Thousands of people listened to him, including around a hundred Muslim scholars. In the sermon, Nursi reflected on major problems of the global Muslim community and offered solutions for them.

In the Islamic tradition, a sermon usually starts with a verse from the Qur'an or a *hadith*, which reflects the core message of the sermon. Nursi followed the tradition by beginning with the qur'anic verse: "Do not despair of God's mercy."[56] This was followed by a *hadith* tradition, stating that the "[Prophet Muhammad] came to perfect morality."[57] At first glance, one might hesitate to see a link between the verse and the *hadith*. The relation becomes clear, though, when one looks at the interpretation of the verse.

In the Qur'an, the whole verse goes as follows: "O my servants who have transgressed against their souls! Despair not of the mercy of God: for God forgives all sins: for he is Oft-Forgiving, Most Merciful." According to the exegete Elmalılı Hamdi Yazır (d. 1942), extravagance does not come only through wasting your property, but also by the acts of transgressing. Extreme sinfulness is also an extravagance, and a crime against one's own soul. This becomes more evident if one takes the specific context of the verse into account. There are various narratives, Elmalılı states, regarding the occasion of revelation (*asbāb al-nuzūl*) of this verse. One refers to Wakhshi who killed Prophet Muhammad's uncle Hamza and who was in doubt over God's forgiveness. The other one points to some of the polytheists (*mushrikūn*) who converted to Islam after torturing and fighting Muslims. They were anxious that God would turn away from them even after having accepted Islam wholeheartedly. As a response to their desperate situation, God sent down this revelation.[58] Like the *hadith*, this verse also deals with morality. In the situation of despair, the only way out is to follow the *sunna*, or the way of the Prophet, in order to find comfort and be saved from that inner turmoil.[59] The Islamic world was in confusion and utter chaos, which led to despair, but living up to Islamic morals based on the Qur'an and the *sunna* would transform the situation into a hopeful state.

56. Qur'an 39:53.

57. Nursi, *Damascus Sermon*, 25.

58. Yazır, *Hak Dini Kur'an Dili*, 4133–34.

59. In Islam, "*sunna*" refers to the way or example of the Prophet. The most important source for the *sunna* is the *hadith*, the reports concerning the Prophet's words and actions. The *sunna* is also an authoritative source for Islamic Law, as the Qur'an instructs the believers to follow the example of the Prophet if they love God. See Qur'an 3:31.

Nursi then diagnosed six sicknesses of the Muslim community. He defined them as despair, deceit, enmity, disunity, despotism, and selfishness. As remedies to these sicknesses, he drew attention to an ideal Muslim displaying the morals of Islam in daily conduct. The following characteristics are identified as elements of this ultimate model.

Considering the tragic condition of the Muslim community, Nursi maintained hope and self-confidence as antidotes for despair. He assured Muslims that a great future is expecting them: "O congregation of Muslims! I give you this good news: the first signs of the true dawn of Arab happiness are just appearing. This happiness will occur through the kindling of the worldly happiness of all Muslims, in particular that of the Ottomans, and especially through the progress of Islam. The emergence of the sun of happiness has drawn close."[60]

Nursi also urged Muslims to be self-confident in practicing their religion. As previously discussed, some of the Ottoman intellectuals attributed the backwardness of the Islamic world to religion. To their mind, Europe's rise and progress was due to parting its way from the Christian faith.[61] Nursi challenged this approach by stating that a parallel reasoning could not be made for Islam. History is a witness that Muslim societies flourished as long as Islam was properly observed. Some of the Muslim leaders, Nursi believed, turned their back to Islam. Therefore, "they fell into savagery and decline, and disaster and defeat amidst utter confusion to the degree of their weakness in adhering to the truths of Islam."[62] Islam cannot be blamed for the failure of Muslims. Its adherents should be self-confident in their religion, even in the most unfortunate times of turmoil and distress.

As for the sickness of deceit within the Muslim community, Nursi offered honesty. He noted that society lacks of truthfulness, which is "the basis and foundation of Islam."[63] For him, in the Era of Bliss, the period of the first Muslim generation, "truthfulness became the most valuable merchandise in the market of human society, and the goods most in demand."[64] This generation of Muslims was inspired by their faith. During their time, there was a great distance between belief and unbelief, as well as between

---

60. Nursi, *Damascus Sermon*, 27.

61. This group of intellectuals is known as the Westernists (*Garpçılar*).

62. Nursi, *Damascus Sermon*, 29.

63. Nursi, *Damascus Sermon*, 45.

64. Nursi, *Damascus Sermon*, 46.

honesty and dishonesty.[65] Over the course of time, however, these distances have drastically been shortened. They gradually got closer. Furthermore, the "political propaganda has sometimes given greater currency to lies, and evil and lying have to some degree taken the stage."[66] For Nursi, truthfulness and honesty were the keys to the salvation of Muslims.[67] This is the most efficient way to revive Islamic morals in the contemporary Muslim world.

Nursi's remedy for enmity in the Muslim world was love. This love was not limited to fellow Muslims. It also embraced the global community at large. He said that the two major world wars ensued because of lack of love. Enmity thus prevailed and the two destructive wars became inevitable. Muslims should embody compassion through their character instead of enmity.

Nursi indicated that people could potentially be destructive and hateful. Yet, if there is anything that is worthy of being hated, it is hatred itself. In this regard, Nursi's motto is "love love and hate hatred."

For the question of conflict, Nursi's solution was unity. Referring to the global Muslim *umma* or community as one family, Nursi stated that a mistake of one individual in the community would affect all its members. Even minor divisions will weaken the strength of the *umma*.[68] He believed that disunity would ultimately contradict with God's order and unity in the universe. Muslims should therefore persistently seek for unity.

Finally, Nursi reflected on the challenge of despotism in his sermon. The remedy should be sought in consultation. He remarked that despotism is one of the major obstacles of being behind the West.[69] For him, "belief necessitates not humiliating others through oppression and despotism and not degrading them, and secondly, not abasing oneself before tyrants. Someone who is a true servant of God cannot be a slave to others. Do not make anyone other than God lord over yourselves."[70] Islam does not leave room for despotism. Consultation is an instrument in order to include

65. Nursi, *Damascus Sermon*, 46.

66. Nursi, *Damascus Sermon*, 46.

67. Nursi, *Damascus Sermon*, 48.

68. Nursi, *Damascus Sermon*, 52–54.

69. Nursi, *Damascus Sermon*, 34.

70. Nursi, *Damascus Sermon*, 56–57.

everyone in the decision-making process. For Nursi, the key for the liberation of the Muslim community lies in "mutual consultation."[71]

What is remarkable about the sermon is that Nursi did not identify any enemy outside of the Muslim community as the cause of its problems. The Christian West is not portrayed to be the scapegoat for the suffering of the Muslim community.[72] Nursi believed that the root cause of all the aforementioned sicknesses is mainly internal. He thus aimed to cure the inner sicknesses. To his mind, the external dimension is simply a reflection of the inner human state since micro- and macrocosmos are strongly related to each other, as the Qur'an confirms. Thus, it is only natural that Nursi saw it as necessary to begin with the inner cosmos and inward transformation as a true means of changing the outer world.

Following his Damascus visit, Nursi was invited by Sultan Mehmed Reşad to accompany him for a trip to Rumelia in 1911. The purpose of the trip was to unite Muslims and non-Muslims alike under the Ottomans in a time when almost all the ethnic subjects of the empire were seeking their independence. Because of his influence, Nursi was asked to be part of the trip on behalf of the eastern provinces.[73]

On his way back to Istanbul, Nursi met two teachers on the train. They had a long discussion regarding the problems of the Ottoman state. With regard to making a choice between the religious and national identity of Muslims, the teachers asked which one should be preferred. The Islamic identity, Nursi answered, is deeply rooted among the Turks and Arabs to the extent that it cannot be separated from them. This identity is a solid illuminating chain ascending to heaven.[74]

Nursi's time in Istanbul after the trip turned out to be brief. He then returned to Van, where he resumed teaching at his *madrasa* and working on the *Medresetü'z Zehra* project until the outbreak of World War I. During the war, Nursi volunteered as a commander, defending the eastern province against the Russian occupation. While fighting at the frontiers, he wrote his qur'anic commentary, *İşaratü'l İ'caz* (*The Signs of Miraculousness*). The commentary only includes the first chapter of the Qur'an, *al-Fatiha* (or "the Opening") and the first thirty-three verses of the second chapter, *al-Baqara* (or "the Cow"). The commentary begins with an introduction, in which

71. Nursi, *Damascus Sermon*, 56–57.

72. Michel, *Said Nursi's Views*, 56.

73. Şahiner, *Bilinmeyen Taraflarıyla*, 131.

74. Vahide, *Islam in Modern Turkey*, 101–2.

Nursi introduced some guidelines for a modern qur'anic commentary. Nursi noted that the Qur'an addresses people of all classes, all ages, and nations in all times. In addition, the Qur'an is highly comprehensive pertaining to sciences. A commentary by one individual alone is therefore unable to do justice in revealing all meanings and implications of the qur'anic verses. One person is limited concerning time, place, and in expertise of all sciences. Nursi pointed out that there is no way for a person to specialize in all sciences. This is beyond the ability of an individual:

> For an individual cannot be acquainted with and be an expert in all the exact sciences and the branches of knowledge concerned with the spiritual and material states of nations and peoples, all of whom the Qur'an addresses. And he cannot be free of bias towards his own profession and discipline that he might explicate the truths of the Qur'an impartially. Also, a person's understanding is peculiar to him and he may not call on others to accept it—unless it is affirmed by a consensus of some sort. And his findings and judgments related to actions are binding only on himself and no one else, again unless approved by a consensus.[75]

Because of an individual's limits, Nursi affirmed, a commentary should be composed by a committee of scholars specialized in different fields. In addition, an individual writing a commentary on the Qur'an should "possess high intelligence penetrating independent judgment, and a high degree of sainthood." In this time, however, Nursi said, such a standard for writing a commentary can only be met by a "brilliant collective personality born of the cooperation of an elevated, esteemed committee and the uniting of the minds of its members, of their assistance for one another and harmony of spirit, and of their freedom of thought, and, being free of bias, of their complete sincerity."[76] Nursi believed that his unfinished commentary could set the tone for further commentaries in the modern time.

During the war, Nursi was arrested as a war prisoner and taken to Kostroma, a riverside city in western Russia. His time in captivity took almost two years. In 1918, Nursi was able to escape and return to Istanbul again. As a reward, he was appointed as the member of *Dar'ul Hikmetü'l İslamiye* (The Academy of Higher Islamic Studies). In Istanbul, he continued to be active. He published some of his works, including *İşaratü'l İ'caz* (the Signs of Miraculousness) which was written in Arabic, and *Mesnevi-i*

75. Nursi, *Signs of Miraculousness*, 14.
76. Nursi, *Signs of Miraculousness*, 14.

Nuriye (The Epitomes of Light), a collection of small treatises, most of which were authored in Arabic.

During his stay in Istanbul, Nursi supported the independence struggle of the nation and issued a *fatwa* in its favor. As an appreciation of his backing for the independence movement, Nursi was invited to the newly established parliament in Ankara at the invitation of Mustafa Kemal Atatürk (d. 1938). Both during his time in Istanbul and Ankara, Nursi witnessed the spread of atheistic and materialistic ideologies in the nation and their influence on leading figures. In addition, in Ankara, he came to realize that the new republic does not consider any role for Islam to play in the new order. Nursi was disappointed. While he was offered to take an active role in the government, Nursi declined. He realized that the Old Said's methods did not bring about any significant change, and he returned to Van. It is believed that his journey from Ankara to Van marked the emergence of the New Said. Before examining Nursi's life in the New Said period, we shall discuss the establishment of the new republic of Turkey, the rise of secularism as well as matters of religious freedom in the new context.

The New Republic and Status of Religious Freedom

No words are better than nationalism, secularism, and westernism at describing the nature of the new republic.[77] Though with a gradual degree, the new republic positioned itself as disconnected from Islam as much as it could. Within the new project for modern Turkey, there was no room for Islam and freedom of religion. In order to make the new state, secular, national, and western reforms were enforced top-down. In contrast to the story of secularism in the United States or Europe, secularism was imposed by "compulsion and without popular consultation."[78] In 1924, the caliphate was abolished. All the religious orders (*tariqas*) were dismantled and their properties were confiscated. Some of the locations of Sufi lodges (*zawiya*)[79] were turned into museums, including some of the mosques. The *madrasas*, or Islamic seminaries, were shut down, and the religious endowments

77. This part is a revised version of a section from one of my articles. For more details see Sayilgan, "Importance of the *Sunna*," 194–97.

78. Ramadan, *Islam and the Arab Awakening*, 76.

79. As the center of Sufi orders, *zawiya* served as a place of worship, social activities, and charity works.

(*waqf*) were seized by the new state.[80] Islamic law was replaced by European law codes.[81]

The new republic also enforced a dress code. Brimless hats, the wearing of which was considered a form of following the *sunna* of the Prophet Muhammad, had been remarkably common among Muslims for centuries. A brimless hat was convenient for Muslim believers, as it could be worn while putting one's forehead on the ground when prostrating during the five daily prayers (*salat*). In the new republic, men were required to wear a brimmed hat, so that Turkey would appear to be part of the civilized world. The fez that had been introduced by Mahmud II (d. 1839)—in fact, any brimless hat—was now forbidden. Also outlawed were all other types of turbans, caps, and other head coverings favored by various groups in the Ottoman Empire—particularly the scholars (*ulama*) and the members of the Sufi orders (*tariqas*).[82] The requirement that hats must have brims was an attempt by the regime to discard Islamic heritage and to replace it with new Western customs.[83] According to Hodgson, the enforcement of the hat law also "served as a psychological *coup*." The idiom "the hatted man" came to mean "a European"; "to put on a hat" meant "to Europeanize," which was taken as synonymous with deserting Islam.[84]

During one of his speeches in Kastamonu, Mustafa Kemal—the founder of modern Turkey—singled out a man in his audience who not only was wearing a fez wrapped with a green turban, but also a traditional smock over which he had donned a modern jacket, saying, "Would a civilized man put on this preposterous garb and go out to hold himself up to universal ridicule?"[85]

The hat law was met with considerable opposition. As historian Carter Findley notes, however, "the independence tribunals (*istiklal mahkemeleri*) repressed their resistance with a reign of 'political-judicial terror,' denying

80. *Waqf* literally means confinement or prohibition. In Islam, it refers to "the holding and preservation of a certain property for the confined benefit of a philanthropy with prohibiting any use or disposition of the property outside that specific purpose." Through such an endowment, the maintenance and expenses of the mosques were provided, the poor were supported, and public institutions were funded. For more details on the *waqf* endowments, see Kahf, "Waqf."

81. Hodgson, *Venture of Islam*, 262.

82. Hodgson, *Venture of Islam*, 264.

83. Hodgson, *Venture of Islam*, 264.

84. Hodgson, *Venture of Islam*, 264.

85. Findley, *Turkey, Islam, Nationalism, and Modernity*, 253.

prisoners legal counsel and overstepping the terms of the penal code."[86] By the time of the closure of the two tribunals in 1927, more than seven thousand people had been arrested and 660 people had been sentenced to death.[87]

Among those who were sentenced to death was Iskilipli Atıf Hoca, a renowned scholar of Islam and a contemporary of Nursi. Known well for his piety, he wore a white beard and a turban while teaching at a *madrasa* or seminary in Istanbul, thus becoming a symbol of the opposition to the hat reform and also the tragedy of Muslims in modern Turkey. One day in December 1925, Atıf Hoca was taken into police custody and then to court. His family learned later that the reason for his arrest was his having authored a booklet, published a year and a half before the hat reform, in which he had criticized those who had adopted the western style of dress. His point had been that Muslims should not blindly imitate the West. To him, while acquiring Western science and technology, Muslims should also preserve their identity.[88] Because his booklet had been written before the hat reform, Atıf Hoca was released initially, but was soon re-arrested by the new regime.[89] After a short trial, he was sentenced to death and was hanged on February 4, 1926.[90]

As a follow-up to the new reforms, Arabic script—that of the Qur'an— was replaced with the Latin alphabet in 1928, and use of the Arabic alphabet in printing was henceforth forbidden. This was a further attempt for the new republic to disconnect itself from both the Ottoman and Islamic heritage. What this ban on the use of the Qur'an's own script accomplished, Hodgson asserts, "was twofold: it ensured that the reform should be psychologically complete and irreversible; and that the younger generation should be abruptly cut off from all the printed books then in the libraries—from the Ottoman literary heritage."[91] The suppression of the Arabic alphabet was accompanied by attempts to remove the Arabic and Persian words in Turkish, replacing them with "French and Gallicized Latin" forms, and giving special attention to words with Turkish origins.[92]

86. Findley, *Turkey, Islam, Nationalism, and Modernity*, 253
87. Findley, *Turkey, Islam, Nationalism, and Modernity*, 253
88. Akyol, *Islam Without Extremes*, 177–78.
89. Akyol, *Islam Without Extremes*, 79.
90. Akyol, *Islam Without Extremes*, 79.
91. Hodgson, *Venture of Islam*, 265.
92. Hodgson, *Venture of Islam*, 265.

It should be nevertheless noted that the new state did not completely dissociate itself from religion. It continued to appoint religious staff, imams, and *muezzins*[93] for the mosques. Yet, the state required that the *ezan* (*adhān*) or the call to prayers be issued in Turkish rather than in Arabic. The form of the *ezan* in Arabic dates to Prophet Muhammad's time, and it is part of his *sunna* or tradition. Requiring the *ezan* to be recited in Turkish was part of the project of nationalizing religion and making it less dependent on Arabic. A more dramatic step was to use some of the mosques as munitions depots.[94] There were even individuals who believed that the more Islam looked like Christianity, the easier it would be to comply with modernity. That is why they proposed that "the mosques should have pews installed, where a congregation would listen to good Islamic preaching rather than focusing on the out-of-date bodily exercises of the *salat* worship."[95]

By the 1940s, the reforms of the new regime were in effect in most cities of Turkey. In his memoirs, Mehmet Kırkıncı (1928–2016), an early follower of Nursi from Erzurum, remarks that in Erzurum all of the *madrasas* and most of the mosques were shut down. The Kurşunlu Mosque, for example, was turned into a prison. Three mosques in Erzurum remained open for worship, but only at certain times. The call to prayer was in Turkish, and the study of the Qur'an and other Islamic sciences were forbidden. In this regard, Kırkıncı notes that he would get up in the early morning and go to the house of his teacher, Hacı Mustafa Efendi, to study the Qur'an and Islamic sciences in secret. Kırkıncı would finish the lesson and return to his house before the police had gotten up and returned to the streets.[96] Although they were very cautious and tried hard not to draw attention to themselves, Kırkıncı narrates, Haci Mustafa Efendi's house was still searched frequently by the police. When the situation became unbearable, the teacher decided to immigrate to Medina, explaining, "I cannot live in this country anymore. I will immigrate. We study our religion here in secret and those who study are imprisoned. The Qur'an is forbidden and there is no *ezan*."[97]

---

93. Technically, *muezzin* means "the one who issues the call to *salat* (ritual prayer)." However, in Turkey during the era being discussed here, the *muezzin* often functioned as a sort of "assistant imam."

94. Zürcher, *Young Turk Legacy*, 267.

95. Hodgson, *Venture of Islam*, 267.

96. Kırkıncı, *Hayatım-Hatıralarım*, 24.

97. Kırkıncı, *Hayatım-Hatıralarım*, 26.

The cultural and educational projects of the new republic were expanded through newly established institutions such as People's Houses (*halk evleri*) and People's Rooms (*halk odaları*), which were extended to the villages. In fact, by the time the People's Houses were closed in 1950, they were about five hundred in number.[98] These houses, open to both children and adults, were significant in spreading various aspects of the new republic's agenda. In order to promote westernization, these institutions would hold activities such as jazz concerts, military band performances, dance courses, and (of course) lessons on the new alphabet.[99]

Perhaps nothing describes the situation of Islam in Turkey's New Republic more eloquently than the title of a book written by German Lilo Linke in the 1930s: *Allah Dethroned: A Journey through Modern Turkey.*[100] We might turn to historian Carter Findley for another perspective on the situation. With all of the reforms, says Findley, "Turkey [moved] closer to the West culturally while moving it further from Western democratic practice."[101] Moreover, the westernizing reforms that moved Turkey away from religious freedom also paved the way for freedom from religion.

The New Said: Exile and Imprisonment

Disillusioned with the New Republic's projects that were at odd with religion in general and with Islam in particular, Nursi avoided involvement in politics after his return from Ankara to Van in 1923. In short, he gave up the methods of the Old Said. Instead, Nursi devoted most of his time to contemplation. He preached on fundamentals of belief rather than on political and social events and developments. Nursi no longer envisioned politics as the means to solve the challenges facing the Muslim community.[102]

It is important to note that, at this time, the eastern province was not very stable. Some of the Kurdish chiefs and sheikhs were not pleased with the new directions taken by the new republic. Several revolts occurred as a result, among them the uprising led by the charismatic Naqshibandi Sheikh Said of Palu in 1925. In fact, because Nursi was a public figure who had many followers and was well-known among Kurds in the eastern part of

98. Findley, *Turkey, Islam, Nationalism, and Modernity*, 255.

99. Findley, *Turkey, Islam, Nationalism, and Modernity*, 255.

100. See Linke, *Allah Dethroned*.

101. Findley, *Turkey, Islam, Nationalism, and Modernity*, 252.

102. Findley, *Turkey, Islam, Nationalism, and Modernity*, 177–78.

Anatolia, Sheikh Said urged him to join in the revolt. With Nursi's support, he believed, the revolt would be successful. Nursi, however, rejected this call. In his reply, Nursi stressed that using the sword was not the solution by saying: "Our only salvation at this time is to offer illumination and guidance through the truths of the Qur'an and belief; it is to get rid of our greatest enemy, ignorance. Give up this attempt of yours, for it will be fruitless. Thousands of innocent men and women may perish on account of a few bandits."[103]

Nursi's response has two elements with particular relevance to our project here. First, he asserts that physical force is not a solution anymore. The best answer is to educate and guide people. Nursi believed in the power of words rather than the power of swords. Second, he notes that innocent people are harmed in the midst of conflicts. For Nursi, a legitimate goal cannot be pursued at the expense of harming innocent people.

Although he did not take part in the revolts, the government was still suspicious of Nursi's influence. Nursi thus was among the many religious and tribal leaders arrested and exiled to western Anatolia in response. Groups of supporters—some of them armed—urged him to allow them to prevent the soldiers from transporting him into exile. Nursi declined their offer, assuring them that his exile was preferable to an outbreak of armed conflict in the region.[104]

For Nursi, this was the beginning of more than thirty years of exile and imprisonment in different parts of Turkey authorized by the new government.[105] He was taken to Istanbul, where he was interrogated about the revolt. During his short time in that city, the new regime's approach to religion became more noticeable to him.

From Istanbul, Nursi was sent to Burdur, a city in southwestern Turkey, where he took up residence in a mosque. The lectures he gave there were collected as *Nur'un İlk Kapısı* (The First Door of Light), and would eventually become the first section of the *Risale-i Nur*. His writings and engagement with people having once again heightened the government's anxiety, Nursi was expelled from Burdur after just a few months. This time, he was sent to Isparta, a neighboring city, where again he attracted students. Alarmed by this, after a mere twenty days, the government moved Nursi again—this time, to the remote mountain village of Barla, accessible only

103. Vahide, *Author of the Risale-i Nur*, 193.

104. Nursi, *Bediüzzaman'ın Tarihçe-i Hayatı*, 151.

105. Turner and Horkuc, *Makers of Islamic Civilization*, 22.

on foot or by horse or donkey. The government's presumption was that, if isolated, Nursi would be forgotten and his influence would fade away.[106] Local people were allowed to visit him occasionally, but the intense surveillance continued—as did the harassment from government officials, who spread rumors and slander about Nursi.[107] Despite these challenges, Nursi's years in Barla proved to be fruitful during his years of exile from 1926 to 1934. Nursi wrote substantial portions of his *Risale* in Barla. At some point, however, the situation in Barla became unbearable.

After Barla, Nursi was taken to Isparta again by government officials, in the hope of inhibiting his ability to receive visitors and communicate with them.[108] Yet, even under police surveillance, Nursi continued to write some parts of *The Flashes* (*Lem'alar*). Eventually, during a search of Nursi's quarters, police found some handwritten books and papers, including a treatise on wearing the head scarf. Nursi and some of his students were then arrested and imprisoned in Isparta. A few months later, having been accused of establishing "a secret society and attempting to change the new regime," he and 120 of his students were taken to a prison in Eskişehir, a city located in northwestern Turkey, where they were held for eleven months.[109]

From Eskişehir, Nursi was exiled to Kastamonu, a city in the northern part of Turkey, for seven years. During his time in Kastamonu, Nursi continued to write. In 1943, Nursi and 126 of his students were arrested again and sent to a prison in Denizli, a city in the southwestern part of Turkey. After nine months there, Nursi and his students were acquitted on all counts. Yet the harassment continued. In 1944, Nursi was exiled to Emirdağ, a town of Afyonkarahisar, where he and fifty-six students were rearrested on charges similar to those from which they had only recently been acquitted. After twenty months of imprisonment in Afyon, Nursi's appeal was again successful; he was acquitted again.

The accusations and court cases would continue until his death in Urfa in 1960. Death did not stop the harassment either, because Nursi's dead body was removed. Today, his graveyard remains empty. State officials removed Nursi's body from it a few months after his burial; the final resting place of his corpse remains unknown. But his legacy is sustained by his *magnum opus*, the *Risale-i Nur*, and its readers.

---

106. Vahide, *Author of the Risale-i Nur*, 198.
107. Vahide, *Author of the Risale-i Nur*, 201.
108. Vahide, "Said Nursi from the Ottoman," 32.
109. Vahide, "Said Nursi from the Ottoman," 33.

Conclusion

Key aspects of the social and political environment in which Nursi lived should now have become clear. First, Nursi's years of formation coincided with the decline of the Ottoman State. Like many other intellectuals of the empire, Nursi sought solutions to save the empire. He started with his own region and proposed a project in order to enact some reforms in the traditional schools of the eastern province of the empire. However, he was unable to fulfill this vision. Second, Nursi cooperated with the Young Turks who initially believed that, to save the empire, some reforms must be made which should be in accordance with Islamic principles. Later on, the Young Turks turned their back to religion and embraced secularization and westernization. Yet, they could not prevent the collapse of the empire. This was Nursi's second disappointment. Third, Nursi took part in the National Independence Movement and supported the establishment of the New Republic. He hoped that the leaders of the new modern Turkey would take Islamic principles as a basis for the new state; however, this did not happen either. Instead, there emerged a secular state with no toleration for anything associated with Islam. The reforms for secularization and westernization were enforced from the top down, and they came in the form of freedom from religion.

Particularly after his visit to Ankara, Nursi realized that, in order to efficiently deal with the problems of Muslim societies, a new approach was necessary. Thus the New Said became visible. The period of the New Said is also a time of exile and imprisonment for Nursi and his students. Yet, even under such severe circumstances, Nursi was able to write his massive qur'anic commentary, the *Risale-i Nur*. Reading and writing became the new means of *jihad* for Nursi and his students, enabling them to remain spiritual as they dealt with the challenges brought about by the new regime and trials of modern times. It is the story of writing the *Risale-i Nur*—the process by which it took form, its dissemination under such severe circumstances, and its structure and contents—to which we now turn.

Chapter 2

The Story of the *Risale-i Nur*

To UNDERSTAND SAID NURSI—to discover the elements of his philosophy of societal transformation via nonviolent means—the *Risale-i Nur Külliyatı* (Epistle of Light Collection)—the Nursi canon—must be our primary source. Nursi's *Risale-i Nur* (henceforth, *Risale*) is a living corpus: Nursi's disciples continue to excerpt it and package it in new ways. It has been deemed a multivolume Qur'an commentary; however, one that is organized topically rather than according to the structure of the Qur'an itself. That is, whereas classic Islamic exegesis proceeds according to verse order, explaining the context of revelation of each verse and offering insights into its meaning, the *Risale* offers reflections on various qur'anic themes and principles. It is a thematic commentary, but unsystematically so, in that the list of themes it addresses is not the governing principle according to which the six thousand pages of text are organized.

Nursi points out that usually there are two types of *tafsīr* or qur'anic exegesis. The first one attempts to explain the message of the verses by focusing on the meaning of the words and verses. With this method, the exegetes of the Qur'an try to derive principles. The second type of *tafsīr*, however, focuses on the foundations of belief and wisdom of the qur'anic truth. It aims to prove and support them.[1] *Tafsīrs* in this category, Nursi indicates, are not uncommon in the tradition. As illustrations, he points to the works of 'Abdul Qādir Jilani (d. 1166), al-Ghazalī (d. 1111), Muhyiddīn ibn 'Arabī (d. 1240), and Ahmad Sirhindi (d. 1624). Nursi also mentions the *Masnavi* of Jalāl al-Dīn Rumi (d. 1273). He considers the *Risale* a spiritual *tafsīr*, similar to their works. Nursi nonetheless asserts that the

---

1. Nursi, *Bediüzzaman'ın Tarihçe-i Hayatı*, 749.

Risale holds a distinctive place among the spiritual *tafsīrs*.[2] In this sense, he frequently emphasizes that the *Risale* belongs to the Qur'an as it is derived from Muslim scripture.

Except for the early treatises which comprise the volume now published as *Mathnawi al-Nuriya* (Epitomes of Light) and *Ishārāt al-I'jaz* (Signs of Miraculousness), all of which were composed in Arabic, the *Risale* was dictated in Ottoman Turkish to disciples during episodes of inspiration, or scrawled by Nursi himself on scraps of paper while imprisoned or under house arrest, without reference in the moment to any external materials, and—it seems—without much in the way of revision. Colin Turner has likened the *Risale* to an edifice—or, perhaps better, to a cluster of buildings. We will better understand its value if we are cognizant of its construction process and structure.[3]

Nursi's *magnum opus* was crafted at the expense of almost thirty years of exile and imprisonment of Nursi and his students, during which reading and writing his *Risale* was considered a major crime and was banned. As was explained earlier, the new modern Turkey of the early twentieth century provided no freedom of religion, no freedom to seek spiritual resources, and no freedom of assembly for religious reasons. Not only did the regime shut down all of the religious institutions, it also began to undermine the tenets of faith in a systematic way through its newly established institutions. In order to cultivate the reforms among Turkish people, the new republic used all means available. In this context, the new institutions that had replaced the old ones and the state-sponsored publications played a significant role, not to mention the psychological pressure that was put on religious people. The state even sponsored the works of some Western intellectuals to be published in Turkish. Among them was French philosopher Baron d'Holbach's (d. 1789) *Le Bon Sens* (Common Sense).[4] As an outspoken atheist, d'Holbach believed that religion was an obstacle for human progress. In the concluding paragraph of *Le Bon Sens*, he writes, "Religion has ever filled the mind of man with darkness, and kept him in ignorance of his real duties and true interest. It is only by dispelling the clouds and phantoms of religion, that we shall discover Truth, Reason, and Morality."[5] In fact, because of his attacks on Christianity, many of d'Holbach's works,

2. Nursi, *İşârâtül-İ'câz*, 379.

3. Turner and Horkuc, *Makers of Islamic Civilization*, 45–46.

4. Hanioğlu, *Atatürk*, 153.

5. d'Holbach, *Good Sense or Natural Ideas*, 140.

including *Common Sense*, "were condemned by the parliament of Paris and publicly burned."[6]

In the face of these challenges, Nursi's reaction was not passive quietism, but a nonviolent reaction, which was an intellectual and rational response. He believed that a physical *jihad* in conflict with the government would not be fruitful; neither did he find any solution in political Islam. By implementing creative civil disobedience, Nursi sought to provide for his community's spiritual welfare.

In the isolated town of Barla, where he had been exiled, Nursi started to deal with the spiritual challenges that had emerged under the new regime by focusing on faith matters. In this environment, contemplation, writing, and reading became the most important means of Nursi's *jihad* or struggle—and these certainly were his most important activities while in Barla. It was there that he wrote some of the major portions of his *Risale*. His first piece, later incorporated into the *Risale* as the Tenth Word, was a treatise making a case for the resurrection of the dead and the afterlife. This being 1926, so early in the process of "modernizing" Turkey, Nursi was able to print a thousand copies of his treatise on resurrection—something that would not be possible to do for his later treatises.

It should be noted that Nursi himself did not have a good handwriting. He therefore described himself as "semiliterate."[7] For the most part, the treatises and other items that would be collected as the *Risale-i Nur* were written down by students in his close circle. These scribes would then make handwritten copies of the original and would distribute them from village to village and town to town in the Isparta area. From there, the treatises would be copied again and, in the course of time, would be spread out throughout Turkey.[8]

Although the first circle of Nursi's students was drawn to him because of his piety, knowledge, and humility, Nursi immediately directed their focus toward his writings. It was Nursi's writings that moved their hearts. We find that attitude expressed by a scribe named Hüsrev Altınbaşak, to whom Nursi referred as the "graceful pen" because of his beautiful handwriting and the dedication of his time to copying the treatises of the *Risale* by hand. In one of his letters to Nursi, Altınbaşak asserted:

6. LeBuffe, "Paul-Henri Thiry (Baron) d'Holbach," para. 5.

7. Vahide, *Islam in Modern Turkey*, 197.

8. Vahide, *Islam in Modern Turkey*, 197.

> Each of your *Words*, that is, your treatises, is a powerful cure. I
> receive great blessings from your *Words*. So much so that the more
> I read them the more I want to read them; I can't describe the
> sublime delight I feel each time I do this. I am certain that anyone
> who reads even one of your *Words* fairly will be obliged to submit
> to the truth; if he is a denier, he will be obliged to give up the way
> he has taken; and if he is a sinner, he will be obliged to repent.[9]

Writing out, studying, and making additional copies of the *Risale* became
the most important task for Nursi's students, which were the new form of
jihad for them. This was the only option for making the *Risale* more accessible. Some of these students rarely left their houses for many years because of their dedication to copying Nursi's works by hand.[10] In the Isparta
area, for example, thousands of the *Risale* students from all classes, men
and women, young and old, were engaged in the project of writing out the
copies of the *Risale*—particularly in the village of Sav, where thousands
of people were involved in the task. For this reason, Sav has been known
among the students of Nursi as the village with a thousand pens.[11] Some of
the women assumed their husbands' responsibilities in order to give their
spouses more time for transcribing copies of the *Risale*. Other women were
scribes themselves. The *Risale* students would also read to each other.[12] The
copying of the *Risale* by hand continued until 1946, when the students of
Nursi were finally able to purchase a duplicating machine. In 1956, Nursi's
students were allowed to print the *Risale* using modern presses and the new
Latin script.[13]

It should be also pointed out that many people who were active in dis-
seminating the *Risale* came to this project unable to read and write. Some of
them learned how to read and write for the first time through their involvement in spreading the message of the *Risale*; others produced *Risale* copies
simply by tracing the letters. Those who were involved in making handwritten copies of the *Risale* did their work under threats from government
officials. Their houses were repeatedly raided and searched for copies of
the *Risale*. For example, when Tenekeci Mehmet, one of Nursi's students in
Isparta, received notification that his house would be searched because of

9. Vahide, *Author of The Risale-i Nur*, 218.

10. Vahide, *Islam in Modern Turkey*, 204.

11. Nursi, *Bediüzzaman'ın Tarihçe-i Hayatı*, 834.

12. Nursi, *Bediüzzaman'ın Tarihçe-i Hayatı*, 205.

13. Vahide, *Islam in Modern Turkey*, 204.

his relationship with Nursi, he immediately buried all of his Nursi treatises in the yard of his house. When the police came, they could not find them.[14] In another instance, in order to preserve the treatises of Nursi, Hafiz Ali hid original copies in his possession in the walls of his house—where they were discovered decades later, after Ali's death.[15]

In fact, many of Nursi's students were imprisoned and tortured for having read or made handwritten copies of the *Risale*. Reading or possessing Nursi's works was a sufficient reason to be imprisoned. While Nursi's followers found strength in reading and studying the message of the *Risale*, governmental intimidation was often severe.[16] In a letter to one of his students in 1934, Nursi describes his situation in Barla as follows: "My brother, the torments of the teacher and chief district officer here have made the situation unbearable. They discomfort me incredibly. I can't even go out into the countryside. I live in my damp room as though living in the grave."[17] To make matters worse, the officials forbade the owner of the little village store from selling any writing materials to Nursi, in the hope of preventing him from writing about matters of faith and spirituality.[18] Thus, even finding such basics as paper and pen became a major issue for Nursi and his students.

From Barla, Nursi was moved to Isparta in 1934, where he wrote several of the treatises that would become part of the *Risale* volume known as *The Flashes* (*Lem'alar*). He remained under strict surveillance, but one of his students was allowed to stay with him. This student who served as a "Nur postman" was Abdullah Kula (d. 1987), known as Abdullah Çavuş, and distributed newly composed treatises to Nursi's followers in secret.[19]

In spring of 1934, along with thirty-one of his students, Nursi was taken to Eskişehir, a city in the north of Isparta, and was imprisoned there. Nursi himself was put in solitary confinement and his students stayed in a ward. While people were arrested because of their genuine connection to Nursi, others, such as Şükrü Şahinler, were deemed guilty by association. In reality, Şahinler had no allegiance to Nursi. He had merely done some business with Halil İbrahim Çöllüoğlu, a Nursi student. The fact that

14. Şahiner, *Son Şahitler*, 2:16–17.
15. Şahiner, *Son Şahitler*, 1:311–12.
16. Vahide, *Islam in Modern Turkey*, 205.
17. Vahide, *Islam in Modern Turkey*, 212.
18. Kırkıncı, *Hayatım-Hatıralarım*, 111.
19. Vahide, *Islam in Modern Turkey*, 212.

Şahinler had exchanged a business letter with Çöllüoğlu was considered a satisfactory reason for him to be imprisoned.[20] Şevket Gözaçan, an optician in Aydın, was caught in a similar situation. Because he had treated the eyes of one of Nursi's students, Nursi had sent him a short letter of thanks. Such a connection was sufficient for the government officials to arrest Gözaçan and send him to Eskişehir Prison.[21]

In a more interesting case, Ahmed Feyzi Kul—who was indeed a Nursi student—had sent a letter to Nursi in Barla and signed it as "The Müftü of Aydın." The signature was a double entendre: Aydın was the name of a city in Turkey, but it also means "the enlightened." Kul intentionally had used the name of Aydın as a joke. But, taking the phrase seriously, the officials arrested the real official *müftü* (the highest religious authority in the city) of Aydın and imprisoned him in Eskişehir, even though he had no connection with Nursi and his students.[22]

Perhaps the oddest arrest was that of a person by the name of Ramazan. While searching the house that Nursi and his students had occupied in Isparta, the police came across Nursi's treatise on the holy month of Ramadan. On the treatise, written in Turkish, were the words "Ramazan'a aittir"—literally, "concerning Ramadan" or "belonging to Ramadan." However, in addition to being the name of the holy month of fasting, Ramazan can be a Turkish person's proper name. Seeing Ramazan on the treatise, the police leapt to the conclusion that the treatise belonged to a person by the name of Ramazan. After a search of the surrounding villages, a person with that name was found and was sent to the prison in Eskişehir. There he was incarcerated for two months, although he had nothing to do with Nursi and his students. The authorities later on admitted their mistake; the person by the name of Ramazan was released.[23]

The conditions endured by Nursi and his students in Eskişehir Prison were harsh:

> Once they entered the prison they were not allowed to visit the lavatories. After hours some warders came and dug a hole near the door and inserted a pipe. This is what they would have to use, they were not to be allowed out. With the filth, the bedbugs, and the cockroaches, it was impossible to sleep at night. For twelve days

20. Şahiner, *Son Şahitler*, 2:73.
21. Şahiner, *Son Şahitler*, 2:73.
22. Şahiner, *Son Şahitler*, 2:73.
23. Şahiner, *Son Şahitler*, 1:364.

they were kept without food. The fact was they were considered to be condemned prisoners doomed for the gallows.[24]

Because he and his students were suffering unjustly during their first imprisonment, Nursi named the prison the School of Joseph (*medrese-i yusufiye*), after the Prophet Joseph who, like them, was imprisoned unjustly. Yet, severe conditions did not stop Nursi from writing. He composed five treatises while in Eskişehir Prison.

Not only did Nursi continue to write, but he also turned the prison into a peaceful place. An informer assigned by the authorities to stay in the ward with Nursi's students described the situation as follows:

> I stayed in the [Nursi] students' ward, so of course I was in close contact with them. It was not possible to think of anything else in those cramped quarters. They held good talks there, the prayers were performed, and the Qur'an recited.
>
> That dark prison ward shone with the lights of the Qur'an. Everyone would rise early for the prayers and take their sections [a thirtieth part] of the Qur'an then the recitations would begin. After the morning-prayer, the prayer for a complete recitation of the Qur'an would be said. From time to time one of the *hojas* with a fine voice [Mehmet Gülırmak] would sing a *kaside*. He used to send us into raptures. Then they would start reciting the Qur'an again. The whole Qur'an was recited several times each day. Those innocent people were saved by the readings of the Qur'an and the prayers. Those were good days. . . . *The prison became like a mosque.* If only I had been able to be like them. There is another thing I witnessed in Eskişehir Prison that has stayed in my mind these fifty years; I always pray for [Nursi's] soul. I had plenty to eat, but he made do with tea and a few olives each day. God's grace was with him; just how great he was, I didn't know.[25]

After eleven months in prison, Nursi was released in 1936. He was sent to Kastamonu, a city in the north of Turkey, where he stayed in exile until 1943. There he continued to add more treatises to his *Risale* collection. Among these pieces was *The Supreme Sign: The Observations of a Traveller Questioning the Universe*. In Kastamonu, Nursi was also able to exchange letters with his students from other parts of Turkey.[26] In the city, Nursi

24. Vahide, *Islam in Modern Turkey*, 217.

25. Şahiner, *Son Şahitler*, 2:69–72 cited in Vahide, *Islam in Modern Turkey*, 219.

26. Later, these letters were incorporated into the *Risale* as the *Kastamonu Lahikası* (Kastamonu Letters).

"spent his time either writing the *Risale-i Nur* or correcting the handwritten copies of existing parts, or in worship, prayer and supplication, or in contemplation."[27] Although approaching Nursi and having a relationship with him would put anyone in trouble, Nursi still attracted new students in Kastamonu. Among them was Çaycı Emin, who was also in exile from the eastern part of Turkey and was now making his living as the proprietor of a tea shop in the yard of the Nasrullah Mosque. Another was Mehmet Feyzi, who became Nursi's scribe. Yet another was Selahaddin Çelebi, from İnebolu, who heard about Nursi, so came to Kastamonu in order to meet him. Çelebi went on to play a significant role in promulgating the *Risale* in his hometown of İnebolu. Nursi had discovered that Çelebi had a beautiful handwriting, so he gave him some *Risale* treatises to copy. Not only did Çelebi make many such copies, he also involved thousands of İnebolu's residents in the project. He remarked that "people's pens worked like printing presses."[28] With the help of the Nur postmen, these handwritten copies were then distributed to other parts of Anatolia from the port of İnebolu.[29]

In other places in Anatolia, shepherds, harvesters, farmers, and nomads would dedicate their time for the continuing project of writing out *Risale* copies and distributing them in secret.[30] Even shepherds, for example, would carry new portions of the *Risale* in their bags and would deliver them to be copied in the places where they stopped regularly.[31] Hüsrev, a Nursi student who had a particularly beautiful handwriting, wrote out four-hundred copies of various treatises of the *Risale* in less than a decade.[32] In one of his letters, Nursi remarks that a previously illiterate elderly person learned how to write after the age of fifty and proceeded to copy forty or fifty pieces from the *Risale*.[33]

Nursi's Kastamonu house was searched many times; eventually, he was rearrested. Initially taken to Ankara and Isparta, Nursi was later sent to Denizli Prison, along with many of his students from different parts of Turkey. The conditions there were even worse than had been the case in the Eskişehir Prison. Nursi was put in a very small cell and kept in solitary

27. Vahide, *Islam in Modern Turkey*, 228.
28. Şahiner, *Son Şahitler*, 2:107–8.
29. Şahiner, *Son Şahitler*, 2:107–8.
30. Vahide, *Islam in Modern Turkey*, 246.
31. Vahide, *Islam in Modern Turkey*, 231.
32. Vahide, *Islam in Modern Turkey*, 231.
33. Vahide, *Islam in Modern Turkey*, 246.

confinement. He was poisoned on many occasions. As had been the case in Eskişehir, with the arrivals of Nursi and his students, Denizli Prison went through a great spiritual transformation. It was in Denizli where Nursi wrote most of his renowned treatise, the Eleventh Ray, *The Fruits of Belief*. Many of the Denizli inmates started to perform the five daily prayers, recite the Qur'an, and assist Nursi in writing out the copies of the *Risale*.[34] They also learned to respect their environment. The cells, for example, were infested with bedbugs, and it had long been the inmates' practice to kill these pests. After their exposure to Nursi's teachings, however, many of them became convinced that, rather being killed, the insects should be collected and thrown out. These inmates bragged that, where once they would have been happy to kill people, because of Nursi's teachings they now could not even kill bedbugs.[35]

The charges against Nursi and his students in Denizli were similar to the ones in Eskişehir. They included "creating a new Sufi tariqa, founding a political society, opposing the reforms, and exploiting religious feelings in a way that might breach public security. The Fifth Ray on *Hadiths* about the end of time, the treatise that had led to the arrests, was the prosecution's main evidence for their alleged exploitation of religion."[36]

In the meantime, the prosecutor formed a committee in order to study the nature of the *Risale*. It only had two high school teachers. They were not qualified to evaluate the *Risale* and write a report. It turned out that their report was full of mistakes and misinterpretations.

Nursi objected to the report and requested a committee of established scholars to evaluate the *Risale* and write a report. Nursi's request was accepted. Under the chief judge of the court, the committee would study Nursi's *Risale* and the exchanged letters with the students.

The report of the committee proved to be positive. It stated that the *Risale* is a scholarly work and does not seek to exploit religion and form a political society. In addition, there is nothing in the *Risale* that would potentially lead to upsetting the social order in the country. However, the committee also highlighted that the "treatises marked as confidential are unscholarly."[37] The report noted that Nursi wrote these unscholarly parts

---

34. Vahide, *Islam in Modern Turkey*, 257.
35. Şahiner, *Son Şahitler*, 2:115.
36. Vahide, *Islam in Modern Turkey*, 260.
37. Vahide, *Islam in Modern Turkey*, 266.

when he was in a state of "mental excitement, ecstasy, or spiritual turmoil."[38] He should thus be "held responsible for them."[39] For example, Nursi wrote about a cat when he believed that the cat was reciting God's name, "the Most Compassionate."[40] The committee also presented some scholarly objections. Based on the report, the court acquitted Nursi and his students. However, the acquittal did not mean freedom. Based on an order from Ankara, Nursi was to reside in a town known as Emirdağ in the province of Afyon. Nursi's exile in Emirdağ continued for seven years; twenty months of this period would be in prison. Meanwhile, Nursi continued his struggle.

Again, the populace was forbidden to approach Nursi. Any connection with him would put anybody at risk. Yet, as it was in other places, Nursi continued to attract new students. Among them were the members of the Çalışkan family, who volunteered to fulfill Nursi's needs. Nursi's Emirdağ's home was in the center of the town, near the police station. The house was guarded by the police, so it was extremely difficult to visit Nursi. The Çalışkan family found a solution for that; they opened a hole from the neighboring shop in order to reach Nursi with provisions. In this situation, Nursi dedicated most of his time to the *Risale*, reading and correcting the copies written out by his students. Here, Nursi completed the last section of *The Fruits of Belief*. With this addition, the *Risale* as a collection was almost complete.

As had happened so many times before, the Turkish authorities, disconcerted by the swift spread of the *Risale* and the steadily increasing numbers of Nursi followers, raided and searched the houses of his students in various parts of Turkey, arrested many, and sent them and Nursi to Afyon prison. Incredibly, conditions there were much worse than in the previous prisons. Nursi's biographer, Şükran Vahide, describes the situation: "Once inside the prison, Nursi was kept in strict isolation. Rules benefiting prisoners were not applied to him. He was allowed no visitors. He was denied assistance with and information about the court proceedings, and to hinder his defense, the public prosecutor held up giving him the Ankara experts' report for six or seven months, though his own forty-six-page indictment was, in part, based on it."[41]

38. Vahide, *Islam in Modern Turkey*, 266.
39. Vahide, *Islam in Modern Turkey*, 266.
40. Vahide, *Islam in Modern Turkey*, 266.
41. Vahide, *Islam in Modern Turkey*, 286.

Yet, despite the severe conditions, Nursi and his students continued to focus on reading and writing the *Risale*, transforming the prison into a school. It was in Afyon where Nursi wrote the last portion of the *Risale*, *Elhüccetü'z Zehra* (The Shining Proof).[42] He also wrote numerous notes and letters to his students, using whatever material he could scavenge—such as the papers from matchboxes. Bayram Yüksel recalls how he and other students of Nursi would assemble in front of Afyon prison to catch notes—some of which were in fact bits of new treatises—that Nursi would throw out of the window to them. They would transcribe these bits and distribute to the other students. This way the new piece would be delivered to different parts of Anatolia.[43]

Nursi was held in Afyon prison for twenty months, with release for him and his students coming in 1949. All legal restrictions on the *Risale-i Nur* were lifted in 1956. From then onward, Nursi's students were able to print his work publicly. It is worth mentioning, nevertheless, that the pressure on the *Risale* and Nursi's students by the state authorities continued until the late 1980s. Nursi died in 1960 in Urfa, a city located in the southeast of Turkey, and was buried there. However, as noted previously, even his dead body was regarded as a threat by the authorities. A few months later, after the military coup of May 27, 1960, Nursi's body was removed from the grave by the military and was taken to a place which remains unknown.

Nursi's legacy is a library, a great collection of treatises written in exile and imprisonment; it is also a community whose hallmark is a deep, systematic study of that library. As we have seen, the *Risale* resulted from the search by Nursi and his students for freedom of religion and ready access to spiritual resources. During their journey, a violent response to persecution was never an option. Nursi's community was committed to positive action and a nonviolent *jihad*. Nursi thus revived the spirit of *jihad* as originally emphasized by the Prophet Muhammad, as will be discussed in greater detail in the next part.

Today, the *Risale* and its readers are Said Nursi's living legacy. The *Risale* continues to provide inspirational guidance for millions—not only in Turkey, but around the globe as well. In the *Risale* and by his personal example, Nursi provided guidelines for positive action for the Muslim community living in a modern secular context of contemporary Turkish Republic. These guidelines are the subject of the next chapter. We will,

42. Vahide, *Islam in Modern Turkey*, 285.

43. Şahiner, *Son Şahitler*, 3:33.

however, begin with a section on the concept of *jihad* and martyrdom in Islam.

PART 2

An Islamic *Jihad* of Nonviolence

Chapter 3

Jihad in Islamic Thought

ISLAM EMERGED IN A milieu where "warfare—or at any rate, armed violence with some degree of organization and planning—was a characteristic of everyday life."[1] The virtue of courage in fighting was a central theme of pre-Islamic Arab literature.[2] Referring to someone as "the son of war" was not uncommon. Those who died while fighting courageously for their people were glorified in poetry after death. The deceased would be praised for "his courage and generosity, and for his steadfast defense of his kin and all those who sought his protection."[3] With the coming of Islam, the virtue of courage merged with the virtue of piety, which came to be known as *jihad*.

The term *jihad*, however, is almost always reduced to a fixed meaning in popular literature. It is often used synonymously with "holy war" or "military/armed combat." While *jihad* as a fight in the path of God became a dominant approach in some contexts in Muslim societies, the concept always had greater implications.

The word *jihad* is derived from the Arabic verb *jahada*, which literally means to endeavor, strive, or struggle. The term *ijtihad*, a key concept in Islamic law, comes from the same root, which means "independent judgment or reasoning in legal or theological questions." Likewise, the word *mujtahid* originates from the same verb. *Mujtahid* is the one who would do diligent reasoning concerning questions in Islamic law.

---

1. Bonner, *Jihad in Islamic History*, 7.
2. Bonner, *Jihad in Islamic History*, 7.
3. Bonner, *Jihad in Islamic History*, 8.

The Qur'an mentions the word *jihad* only twenty-four times, and in most cases the context is spiritual struggle. While it is true that, in the Qur'an, *jihad* has the implication of physical fight, the word does not have any indication for "holy war." Instead, the Qur'an utilizes *qital* for "physical fight." "Holy war" does not exist as a concept in Islamic literature. Warfare or fighting is either just or unjust but never holy. The Qur'an and Islamic law are concerned about the preservation of life. In the qur'anic world, peace is always preferred to conflict "for peace is best."[4] On the basis of the Qur'an and prophetic example, Muslim scholars concede that Islamic law gives pride of place to five universal principles. These are "protection of life, mind, religion, property and offspring."[5] In this regard, killing someone or taking one's own life has never been presented as sacred in Islam.

Jihad is one of the most comprehensive terms in Islamic literature. It means to live in a way that is pleasing to God. Meeting this goal requires struggle and submission. Following the teachings of the Qur'an and *sunna* of the Prophet is *jihad*. Establishing the five daily prayers could be an important *jihad* for a believer, as it is not easy to do so in an environment with many distractions. Giving charity might be another form of *jihad*. For a social worker, taking care of the needy is a form of *jihad*. The *jihad* of a firefighter is to save lives. For the student, seeking knowledge is a *jihad*. According to a *hadith*, the Prophet Muhammad once said that "On the day of resurrection, the ink of scholars will be compared with the blood of the martyrs on the scales and the former will prove to be higher in status."[6]

Sabr or patience also became an essential component of *jihad* in Islamic literature. Both the Qur'an and *hadith* urge the believers to have patience in the face of challenges to their faith, persecution, and aggression. This becomes particularly evident in the Qur'an: "Say, '[God says], believing servants, be mindful of your Lord! Those who do good in this world will have a good reward—God's earth is wide—and those who persevere patiently will be given a full and unstinting reward.'"[7] The point is that God will eventually reward the virtue of patience.

Perhaps the best example from the life of the Prophet concerning the connection between patience and *jihad* is the Treaty of Hudaybiyya. A

4. Qur'an 4:128.

5. Hallaq, *Introduction to Islamic Law*, 26.

6. al-Ghazāli, *Ihyā' 'Ulūm al-Dīn*, 19 and 22. See al-Suyuti, *al-Jami' al-Saghir*, no: 10026.

7. Qur'an 39:10.

major event in the life of the nascent Muslim community during its formative years, this was an accord between the Prophet Muhammad's followers
and his enemies in Mecca, established in the sixth year of the *hijra* (628 CE).
The Prophet and his followers were set out to perform their pilgrimage.
Given that it was during the sacred months, no conflict was expected. Meccans had respected the sacred months as well. The Muslim community was
now an important force challenging Mecca. According to this agreement,
they would have peace for ten years. The treaty also granted the Prophet
Muhammad and his followers to do their pilgrimage the next year. It also
included a challenging agreement between the two parties. According to
the deal, if a young man would convert to Islam and be part of Muhammad's community, he would be returned. However, if anyone would decide
to leave the Muslim community and go back to the Meccans, this person
would not be returned. The companions of the Prophet were devastated at
this agreement. They found it unfair and unjust. The treaty eventually yielded good results for Muslims. Later on, they were able to enter Mecca to do
their pilgrimage and conquer their enemy's heart without any bloodshed.

The *hadith* collections usually include a section on the virtue of *jihad*.
In one of them, the Prophet remarks that a *mujahid*, or the person who
does *jihad*, is the one who deals with his lower self or ego. Addressing a
question from his wife Aisha, the Prophet said, "for you the best form of
jihad is to perform your *hajj* or pilgrimage."[8] In another *hadith*, Muhammad said, "the best *jihad* is to speak the truth before a tyrannical ruler."[9]

On another occasion, the Prophet and his companions were returning from a major battle. He told them that "you have returned from the
lesser struggle (*jihad*) to the greater struggle." Muslims have interpreted
the Prophet's statement as returning from physical fighting to a spiritual
struggle. Muhammad also said, "Shall I tell you of your best deed, the most
pleasing to your King, the loftiest in your ranks, better than the giving of
gold and silver, and better than meeting your enemy in battle, beheading
him whilst he beheads you? The remembrance of God."[10]

In the literature, Muslim scholars speak of multiple categories of *jihad*.
In his book *Zād al-Ma'ad*, Ibn Qayyim al-Jawzīyyah (d. 1350) mentions
fourteen—among them, *jihad* with heart, tongue, and wealth, and against
self. Only one of these categories refers to outward *jihad*. Similarly, in his

---

8. *Sunan an-Nasa'i*, 2628. Also see Dağlı, "Conquest and Conversion," 1806.

9. *Jami' at-Tirmidhi*, 2174. Also see Dağlı, "Conquest and Conversion," 1806.

10. *Jami' at-Tirmidhi*, 3377. Also see Dağlı, "Conquest and Conversion," 1806.

Muqaddimah, Ibn Rushd (d. 1198), known as Averroes in the West, talks about four types of *jihad*: by the heart, tongue, hand, and sword. The concept of *jihad* has therefore never had to do with outward violence alone.

Nevertheless, one cannot dismiss the violent aspect of *jihad*. Muslim scholars acknowledge that the struggle might also be in the outward form against the threats to Muslims or Islam. This type of *jihad* might be violent and could involve wars. During Prophet Muhammad's thirteen years in Mecca, he and his companions were forbidden to use any violent means, although they were severely persecuted. As a result, some of his followers immigrated to Abyssinia as refugees. The major principle in this period in dealing with the enemy was to "turn the other cheek." However, this approach changed when they immigrated to Medina. In one chapter of the Qur'an, God permits Muslim believers to fight:

> Those who have been attacked are permitted to take up arms because they have been wronged—God has the power to help them—those who have been driven unjustly from their homes only for saying, "Our Lord is God." If God did not repel some people by means of others, many monasteries, churches, synagogues, and mosques, where God's name is much invoked, would have been destroyed. God is sure to help those who help His cause—God is strong and mighty—those who, when We establish them in the land, keep up the prayer, pay the prescribed alms, command what is right, and forbid what is wrong: God controls the outcome of all events.[11]

The Qur'an also includes verses that are frequently incorporated into the rhetoric of Muslim extremists and critics of Islam. One of them is Qur'an 9:5: "When the [four] forbidden months are over, wherever you encounter the idolaters, kill them, seize them, besiege them, and wait for them at every lookout post."[12] Although the Qur'an does not employ the word "sword," this verse is often called the "sword verse." This verse is intentionally selected by the critics of Islam, arguing that Islam is an inherently violent religion. Ironically, as noted by John Esposito, the same verse is picked by some Muslim extremists. By twisting the overall message of the Qur'an, they attempt "to develop a theology of hate and intolerance and to justify unconditional warfare against unbelievers."[13] Both camps distort the

11. Qur'an 22:39–41.

12. Qur'an 9:5.

13. Esposito, *What Everyone Needs to Know*, 138.

implication of the verse, as the reference is to the Meccan unbelievers and their allies who were breaking their treaty with Muslims and continuously waging war on them.[14] They also completely disregard the second part of the verse, in which the Qur'an instructs the believers as follows: "but if they turn [to God], maintain the prayer, and pay the prescribed alms, let them go on their way, for God is most forgiving and merciful."[15] Even in this verse, which has a particular context, the Qur'an favors peace and reconciliation over war and conflict.

In truth, as with any religious community, war and violence have been part of Muslim societies from the beginning. The Prophet said: "O people! Do not long to encounter the enemy and ask God to grant you safety and security. However if you face them be patient and know that the heaven lies under the shadow of the swords."[16] Prophet Muhammad himself participated in many wars. After his death, Muslims were involved in many battles and embarked on journeys of conquests and expeditions. It should be noted that such an approach was part of almost all religious societies in the milieu in which Islam emerged. In this environment, two major empires, the Byzantine and the Sasanian, were in religious war because of "territorial expansion."[17] In addition, it is worth remembering that religion was not only about individual spirituality, but also identity in that context. Reza Aslan puts this aspect of religion as the following:

> Your religion was your ethnicity, your culture, and your social identity; it defined your politics, your economics, and your ethics. More than anything else, your religion was your citizenship. Thus, the Holy Roman Empire had its officially sanctioned and legally enforced version of Christianity, just as the Sasanian Empire had its officially sanctioned and legally enforced version of Zoroastrianism. In the Indian subcontinent, Vaisnava kingdoms (devotees of Vishnu and his incarnations) vied with Saiva kingdoms (devotees of Shiva) for territorial control, while in China, Buddhist rulers fought Taoist rulers for political ascendancy. Throughout every one of these regions, but especially in the Near East, where religion explicitly sanctioned the state, territorial expansion was identical

14. Esposito, *What Everyone Needs to Know*, 138. See also Nasr et al., *Study Qur'an*, 506–7.

15. Qur'an 9:5.

16. *Sahih Muslim*, 4542, and *Sahih al-Bukhari*, 3025.

17. Aslan, *No God But God*, 80.

to religious proselytization. Thus, every religion was a "religion of the sword.[18]

There were occasions in Islamic history when the discourse of *jihad* provided an ideological basis for the territorial expansion. For example, as Khalid Blankinship explains, "[The Umayyad] caliphate constituted the *jihad* state par excellence. Its main reason for existence, aside from maintaining God's law, was to protect Islam and to expand the territory under its control, and its reputation was strongly bound to its military success."[19] With territorial expansions and conquests, Muslims were then faced with the challenge of the ethics of conducting war. It is within this framework that Muslim scholars began to put forward a theory of *jihad*. Before the theory, as noted by Carole Hillenbrand, "Muslim scholars and judges had tried to make judgments not only with pragmatism and common sense but also, above all, in a true spirit of piety and with a sincere desire to follow qur'anic principles and the model conduct of the Prophet."[20]

It is particularly during the Abbasid dynasty that Muslim scholars wrote extensively on *jihad*, developing a classical Islamic legal theory in the process. One of the earliest examples is 'Abdallah Ibn Mubarak's *The Book of Jihad* (d. 797).[21] Muslim jurists of this era divided the world into two abodes: the abode of Islam (*dar al-Islam*) and the abode of war (*dar al-harb*). The former referred to the lands ruled by Muslims, and according to Islamic law, the abode of Islam could also include Christians and Jews. These groups would be protected under Muslim rule; however, their status would still be inferior to Muslims. They were also subjected to "certain social and religious restrictions."[22] In some cases, when the context changed, religious groups such as Zoroastrians, Hindus, and Buddhists enjoyed a similar protection under Muslim rule.

The abode of war, on the other hand, referred to the lands that were ruled by non-Muslims, or the places where Muslims lived as minorities—thus, Islamic law was not the law of the land. Occasionally, a Muslim caliph would call for a *jihad* against the abode of war. In accordance with Islamic law, people of that region would be invited first to accept Islam. If they agreed, the war would end. The other option for them was to "submit to

18. Aslan, *No God But God*, 80.

19. Blankinship, *End of the Jihad State*, 232.

20. Hillenbrand, *Introduction to Islam*, 223.

21. Hillenbrand, *Introduction to Islam*, 224.

22. Hillenbrand, *Introduction to Islam*, 224.

Muslim rule and pay the poll tax."[23] Some Muslim scholars later on in-troduced another category known as the abode of truce (*dar al-'ahd*) or the abode of peace (*dar al-sulh*).[24] Based on this territorial classification, a Muslim state can be in contract with another state regardless of their reli-gious status.[25]

The classical legal theory of *jihad* introduced regulations for peace treaties, as well as proper ethics of war. According to the new guidelines, combatants and non-combatants were to be treated differently. For ex-ample, children, women, clergy of any religious tradition, and the elderly would be considered noncombatants, and thus were not to be harmed. The law was later expanded to "outlaw the torture of prisoners of war; the muti-lation of the dead; rape, molestation, or any kind of sexual violence during combat; the killing of diplomats, the wanton destruction of property, and the demolition of religious or medical institutions."[26] These regulations eventually made their way into the modern international law.[27]

As Islamic thought continued to develop, scholars of Islamic law took a range of positions on *jihad*, with context playing a significant role in their interpretation.[28] In this regard, one needs to mention the perspective of Ibn Taymiyyah (d. 1328). During the era of his intellectual activity, Mus-lims were dealing with a dual threat: crusaders from the West and Mongols from the East. By the end of the thirteenth century, the crusaders had been expelled from their kingdom in Syria. The Mongols' destructive influence continued, however. In 1258, they destroyed Baghdad, the center of the Abbasid Caliphate, as well as Islamic civilization. While the Mongols even-tually converted to Islam, this created a further dilemma: these converts would not relinquish all of their cultural practices, particularly their *ya-sas*—their own legal code.

Within this environment, Ibn Taymiyyah feared that too many su-perstitions had embedded themselves in Muslim societies as a result of interactions with Christian and Mongol practices. As he saw it, while the formerly pagan Mongols had become Muslim, they still had kept their *ja-hiliyya* practices. He also criticized the Shiites of his time for collaborating

23. Hillenbrand, *Introduction to Islam*, 225.

24. Hillenbrand, *Introduction to Islam*, 225.

25. Hillenbrand, *Introduction to Islam*, 225.

26. Aslan, *No God But God*, 80.

27. Aslan, *No God But God*, 80.

28. Afsaruddin, *Striving in the Path of God*, 94.

with the Mongols. Thus, says Hillenbrand, Ibn Taymiyyah "condemned many practices and concepts—visiting graves, the veneration of saints, sharing religious festivals with other faiths, theology, philosophy, ostentatious dress, backgammon, chess, and music."[29] He eventually came to the conclusion that *jihad* against them was a religious obligation.[30] Ibn Taymiyyah's interpretation of *jihad* has had a significant impact on some of the modern Islamic movements, especially among Wahhabis and Salafis.[31] Muhammad abd-al-Salam Faraj and Osama bin Laden both drew significantly on Ibn Taymiyyah's legal thoughts in justifying violence against civilians in the name of religion.[32]

With the decline and stagnation of the Muslim world in the early eighteenth century, *jihad* took a different turn. The notion of *jihad* would serve to tackle the challenges of Muslim societies. In some situations, it has been a form of resistance against colonialism; in other contexts, it has been a means to promote nationalism.[33] A more distinctive interpretation of *jihad* emerged as a response to the challenges of Muslim societies in the early twentieth century. As noted by Asma Afsaruddin, during that era, *jihad* became "a means effecting sociopolitical reform in Muslim-majority societies by the removal (with violence and other means) of indigenous authoritarian, secular governments"[34]—a model of *jihad* that had not been employed in the pre-modern period.

This model of legitimate struggle against a Muslim government was unusual because, in Islamic law traditionally, rebellion against a lawful Islamic authority had been regarded as a *baghy* (rebel), and thus was strongly discouraged. In fact, it was regarded as a major crime defined as *hiraba*—a word that carries a connotation similar to today's terrorism. As rightly put by Afsaruddin, "armed uprising against a well-entrenched government, however tyrannical it might be perceived to be, was usually not justified under the rubric of *jihad* in the pre-modern period. This development alone marks a radical departure from pre-modern juridical and political thought."[35]

29. Hillenbrand, *Introduction to Islam*, 223.
30. Hillenbrand, *Introduction to Islam*, 223.
31. Afsaruddin, *Striving in the Path of God*, 200.
32. Afsaruddin, *Striving in the Path of God*, 216 and 220.
33. Hillenbrand, *Introduction to Islam*, 223.
34. Afsaruddin, *Striving in the Path of God*, 205.
35. Afsaruddin, *Striving in the Path of God*, 206.

In any discussion of *jihad*, another term deserving our attention is *shahid* ("martyr"). Like *jihad*, this concept has various connotations in Islamic literature. It is derived from the Arabic verb *shahida* ("to witness"; "to testify"). In the Qur'an, the word *shahid* also appears as one of God's Beautiful Names (*asma al-husna*). In some qur'anic contexts, *shahid* refers to someone who is a model or an example in living according to God's will: "We have made you [believers] into a just community, so that you may bear witness [to the truth] before others and so that the Messenger may bear witness [to it] before you."[36]

A *hadith* of Prophet Muhammad explains that *shahid* might have many different implications. According to this tradition, the Prophet visited one of his companions who was ill. When he entered the companion's house, he saw that the companion's mother was crying because of her son's illness. Muhammad then turned to her and said, "You think that one can only become martyr while fighting in the path of God. In that case your martyrs would be few." The Prophet then stated that "being killed in the path of God is martyrdom, dying of an abdominal complaint is martyrdom, being burned to death is martyrdom, drowning is martyrdom, being crushed beneath a falling wall is martyrdom, dying of pleurisy is martyrdom, and the woman who dies along with her fetus is a martyr."[37]

In relation to military *jihad*, the term *shahid* is understood as a witness or martyr who lays down his life for the religion of Islam. The Qur'an refers to those who barter their life and wealth in exchange for the rewards in the hereafter: "God has purchased the persons and possessions of the believers in return for the Garden—they fight in God's way: they kill and are killed—this is a true promise given by Him in the Torah, the Gospel, and the Qur'an. Who could be more faithful to his promise than God? So be happy with the bargain you have made: that is the supreme triumph."[38] In another verse, the Qur'an says, "Let those of you who are willing to trade the life of this world for the life to come, fight in God's way. To anyone who fights in God's way, whether killed or victorious, We shall give a great reward."[39]

According to Afsaruddin, while the word *shahid* has broad connotations, in the course of time and with the influence of social historical

---

36. Qur'an 2:143.
37. *Sunan an-Nasa'i*, 3194.
38. Qur'an 9:111.
39. Qur'an 4:74.

context, the interpretation of martyrdom that "privileged the military martyr over all other believers" came to predominate.[40] Along with the concept of *jihad*, the concept of martyrdom makes a frequent appearance in the literature promoting extremism. Even modern secular Muslim states called their fallen soldiers "martyrs."

As shown, the concepts of *jihad* and martyrdom have had many different connotations and interpretations in Islamic literature over the centuries. These concepts were never reduced solely to fighting and violence. They encompassed many aspects of Islamic spirituality, including worship and charity. In some contexts, however, *jihad* as an effort to wage war has become the principal interpretation, both in pre-modern and modern times. One can observe a similar evolution for the concept of martyrdom. In this regard, there have been occasions that both concepts served as means for political agendas. In these situations, as Murata and Chittick note, there would be scholars who would "lend support to the king—such as the scholar whom the king had appointed to be chief preacher at the royal mosque."[41] It is also important to state that there have been scholars who would not sanction a war as a *jihad* simply because the king said so. "They would only support those that followed the strict application of Islamic teachings. By these standards, it is probably safe to say that there have been few if any valid *jihads* in the past century, and perhaps not for the past several hundred years."[42] We now turn to Said Nursi's method of positive action (*müsbet hareket*) which is an important component of his understanding of a *jihad* of nonviolence

40. Afsaruddin, *Striving in the Path of God*, 114.
41. Sachiko and Chittick, *Vision of Islam*, 22.
42. Sachiko and Chittick, *Vision of Islam*, 22.

Chapter 4

Foundation of *Jihad* of Nonviolence:
Positive Action

Diagnosing the Problem

As SHOWN IN CHAPTER 1, in the first phase of his life, Said Nursi sought new ways to prevent the decline of the Ottoman Empire and the Muslim world in general. However, the empire collapsed. The new secular establishment of the Turkish Republic considered the religion of Islam as a major obstacle to progress and improvement, and thus took steps to remove religion from the public sphere. The major institutions providing religious education and spiritual nurture were eliminated. The right to hold religious gatherings and to engage in communal worship outside of state control was eliminated. Following the Prophet Muhammad's *sunna* (his example) was no longer possible.

More than anything, the republic's elimination of the religious institutions created a spiritual gap exacerbated by state-sponsored scientific materialism, aggressive secularism, and positivism. In short, the republic was determined to keep people away from religious practice and to diminish their faith. Faced with these conditions, Nursi and his followers did not remain passive. Rather, they sprang into action to combat the new republic's foundational ideologies by means of nonviolent resistance.

In seeking solutions for the Muslim community, some scholars and popular movements have invested in the external aspects of religion such as politics and *sharia* (Islamic law). They believed that, with the right

53

environment and government, it was possible to solve the problems of the Muslim community.[1] Nursi, however, thought otherwise. In his *Risale*, Nursi remarks that there are three important stages for the Muslim community concerning Islam. The first one is faith (*iman*). The second one is the embodiment of faith in individual and social lives or in public (*hayat*). When the first stage is strong, naturally faith (*iman*) in practice becomes more visible in the lives of people. The third stage is *sharia* (*şeriat*). Because of the strength of the first two stages, Islam and its principles would become organically more influential in politics and government. While many Muslims focus most on the second and third stages, for Nursi the first stage, faith (*iman*), was the priority and the only goal.[2] As noted by Şerif Mardin, "in contrast to al-Ghazālī, Nursi did not dwell much on the areas of Islamic social relations and forms of worship, but studied the areas that would assist Muslims in understanding their own religion . . . Muslims need a 'map' to give them direction in their own daily lives. Nursi understood this."[3] This map was addressing the new challenges to the Muslim community in Turkey. In fact, the map did not merely aim to tackle the problems in modern secular Turkey. Nursi had a bigger vision. His map was addressing "the more encompassing problems of industrial civilization and its basis in rationalist philosophy. Nursi continuously dwells on meaning and presents Islam as a religion that must be understood. In his writings, one can see that Nursi understood the dilemma to be worldwide and not just a problem of Turkey."[4] For him, belief in the lives of people and *sharia* are the manifestations of faith. Furthermore, in his views, a society cannot fix faith—in practice in the lives of the believers—and *sharia* simultaneously. It is just not possible.[5] In this sense, therefore, Nursi's concern was not to establish an Islamic state, but an Islamic state of mind and heart. He believed that many problems of the *umma* stemmed from the weakness of faith.

In diagnosing the problem, Nursi repeatedly makes a case for faith in God. It was his firm conviction that faith in God is the most important aspect of creation and that it is through belief that people can have meaning and happiness:

1. Modern Muslim movements such as the Muslim Brotherhood and the Salafi Movement are two examples.

2. Nursi, *Kastamonu Lahikası*, 116.

3. Mardin, "Reflections on Said Nursi's Life," 49.

4. Mardin, "Reflections on Said Nursi's Life," 49–50.

5. Mardin, "Reflections on Said Nursi's Life," 49–50.

Be certain of this, that the highest aim of creation and its most important result is belief in God. The most exalted rank in humanity and its highest degree is the knowledge of God contained within belief in God. The most radiant happiness and sweetest bounty for jinn and human beings is the love of God contained within the knowledge of God. And the purest joy for the human spirit and the sheerest delight for man's heart is the rapture of the spirit contained within the love of God. Yes, all true happiness, pure joy, sweet bounties, and untroubled pleasure lie in knowledge of God and love of God; they cannot exist without them. The person who knows and loves God Almighty may receive endless bounties, happiness, lights, and mysteries. While the one who does not truly know and love him is afflicted spiritually and materially by endless misery, pain, and fears. Even if such an impotent, miserable person owned the whole world, it would be worth nothing for him, for it would seem to him that he was living a fruitless life among the vagrant human race in a wretched world without owner or protector. Everyone may understand just how forlorn and baffled is man among the aimless human race in this bewildering fleeting world if he does not know his Owner, if he does not discover his Master. But if he does discover and know Him, he will seek refuge in His mercy and will rely on His power. The desolate world will turn into a place of recreation and pleasure; it will become a place of trade for the hereafter.[6]

It is fair to say that the whole mission of the *Risale* is to bring about this vision to people's lives. God is in the center of such a life. Challenging the ideological threats to faith thus becomes the most important goal of Nursi and his *Risale*: "I have only one objective. In the time in which I am close to the grave, I hear the voices of Bolshevik owls in the Muslim lands. These voices harm the foundational belief of the Muslim world. They attract youth by promoting non-belief. With all of my strength, I am dealing with this problem and inviting Muslims to belief. I am working against the community that promotes unbelief."[7]

Nursi was concerned about excessive materialism, asserting that constant focus on worldly things distracts believers from the hereafter and weakens their faith. However, the greatest threat facing Muslims of his era, he insisted, was scientific materialism and positivism, which corrupts their hearts and harms their belief. As Nursi saw it, the "castle" of belief was in

6. Nursi, *Letters*, 265.
7. Nursi, *Şu'alar*, 618.

danger—but from a threat unlike any previous one. In ages past, Nursi observed, unbelief was rare; unbelievers were one in a thousand. The reason for unbelief would have been ignorance; therefore, to rectify it was a simple matter.

Today, believers live in a different context. In his renowned book *The Secular Age*, Charles Taylor sheds light on this new context to understand religion in a secular age. Taylor points out that "it was virtually impossible not to believe in God in, say, 1500 in our western society, while in 2000 many of us find this not only easy but even inescapable."[8] He describes the transition as "a move from a society where belief in God is unchallenged and indeed, unproblematic, to one in which it is understood to be one option among others, and frequently not the easiest to embrace."[9]

Referring to the context of Western society, Taylor points out that "we have undergone a change in our condition, involving both an alteration of the structures we live within, and our way of imagining these structures."[10] Some of the structural changes manifested in forms of "scientific, social, and technological" frame. Such a frame, Taylor indicates, is "natural or this-worldly," which may not necessarily require a reference to the "supernatural" or "transcendent."[11] As a result, Taylor concludes that a change in Western society "has destabilized and rendered virtually unsustainable earlier forms of religious life, but that new forms have sprung up."[12]

Like Taylor, Nursi believed that, within these new circumstances, a new narrative of faith needs to be offered in order to cope with the challenges of time. In a sense, Nursi wanted to put forward a religious account of Islam that would be compatible with the spirit of the age in which unbelief was promoted through sciences.[13] Nursi was convinced that faith under attack within a scientific framework is best bolstered by employing methods calling attention to the benefits of science.

While seeking creative ways for realizing his vision, Nursi made the notion of positive action (*müsbet hareket*) the most important aspect of his mission, and thus puts forth practical guidelines for implementing it. The goal of positive action is always to build or mend what is destroyed

8. Taylor, *Secular Age*, 26.
9. Taylor, *Secular Age*, 3.
10. Taylor, *Secular Age*, 594.
11. Taylor, *Secular Age*, 594.
12. Taylor, *Secular Age*, 594.
13. Nursi, *Mektubat*, 48.

or corrupted; destruction or corruption is never an option. As we saw in chapters 1 and 2, even under the severest of conditions, Nursi and his students preferred positive action—the most important element of his nonviolent resistance.[14] As a methodology, nonviolent resistance strives to avoid harming people.[15] In bringing his vision to fruition, Nursi believed that political Islam was not the means by which necessary change would be brought; changing the regime and establishing a *sharia*-based government were not his concerns either. Rather, he focused on matters of faith and the transforming of individuals. In this endeavor, nonviolent positive action becomes Nursi's form of *jihad*.

Positive Action's First Step: Forming Positive Perspectives

The basis of Nursi's method of nonviolent positive action is prevention. Throughout his *Risale*, his purpose is to form Islamic—that is, faithful— minds and hearts. For Nursi, forming positive perspectives is a point of departure for forming faith-filled individuals in a modern secular environment. Such a change must start from within. Once affected, it will prevent the encroachment of secularism. In what follows, some of Nursi's guidelines for forming positive perspectives should be presented.

See Beautifully; Think Beautifully

Destructive behaviors are the embodiment of crises in mind and heart, and are also in many cases the causes of external problems. The proponents of nonviolence, for example, focused on mental tools such as meditation that can help individuals to direct their consciousness from violence toward peace or nonviolence.[16]

This is also part of Nursi's positive action method (*müsbet hareket*). Nursi thus endeavors to build from the inside out. His assertion that "the one who sees beautifully thinks beautifully; thinking of what is good makes life pleasant,"[17] has become a mantra for his students. Embedded in it is the idea that both the macrocosm and the microcosm are the mirrors of God's

14. Vanderhaar, *Active Nonviolence*, 10.

15. Vanderhaar, *Active Nonviolence*, 10.

16. Kunkel, "Spiritual Side of Peacemaking," 35.

17. Nursi, *Mektubat*, 669.

attributes. All the elements in the universe reflect God's Beautiful Names (*asma al-husna*). Although one can observe such cosmology throughout Nursi's *Risale*, his *Ayetü'l Kübra* (The Supreme Sign) is entirely dedicated to reading the elements of the universe with awe and admiration. This treatise is a testimony of one curious and observant traveler who wonders about the heavens, the earth, the seas and rivers, the mountains and plains, and the trees and plants, amongst human beings, birds, angels and other spirits, and more. Through the eyes of this traveler, Nursi explores beauty in all realms of the universe. In the section on the earth, for example, the traveler offers this meditation:

> The forms of the countless members of hundreds of thousands of species emerge, in the utmost precision, from a simple material and are then nurtured in most merciful fashion. Then, in miraculous manner, wings are given to some of the seeds; they take to flight and are thus dispersed. They are most effectively distributed, most carefully fed and nurtured. Countless tasty and delicious forms of food, in the most merciful and tender fashion, are brought forth from dry clay, and from roots, seeds and drops of liquid that differ little among each other. Every spring, a hundred thousand kinds of food and equipment are loaded on it from an unseen treasury, as if onto a railway wagon, and are despatched in utmost orderliness to animate beings. The sending to infants of canned milk in those food packages, and pumps of sugared milk in the form of their mothers' affectionate breasts, is in particular such an instance of solicitousness, mercy and wisdom that it immediately establishes itself as a most tender manifestation of the mercy and generosity of the Merciful and Compassionate One.[18]

Thus, the beauties on the earth are recalled in a way that reminds us of the Sustainer, the Merciful and Compassionate One. In this portrait of the earth, nothing is extraneous: everything has a divinely ordained purpose.

In another instance, Nursi refers to the earth as "the garden of the universe." In his description, again the mantra of "see beautifully, think beautifully" prevails:

> Look at this garden of the universe, this orchard of the earth; look carefully at the beautiful face of the heavens gilded with stars! You will see that on all the artifacts spread out and scattered over them are stamps particular to the Creator of All Things, and on all creatures are seals special to the Maker of All Things, and on the levels

18. Nursi, *Rays*, 135.

of being written on the pages of night and day, and summer and winter, all published by the pen of power, are inimitable, illustrious signatures of an All-Glorious Maker, an All-Beauteous Creator.[19]

In his *Mathnawi*, Nursi states that, throughout his life and in thirty years of his education, he learned four words: seeing the meaning beyond what is apparent (*mana-yı harfi*); seeing what is apparent (*mana-yı ismi*); intention (*niyet*), and perspective (*nazar*). In fact, all four are about right perspective or thinking.[20] Nursi points out that one should look at every single element as the sign of God and see the meaning behind its creation. Just seeing what is apparent without remembering who created it is a grave mistake.[21]

A simple analogy may help us to understand these two different perspectives. Let's imagine that one is taking an exhibition tour of Picasso's art. While one would greatly enjoy the artworks, it is important that one remembers that the artist of these artistic works is Picasso. What brings the observer into awe is both the work of art and the artist behind it. Analogously, Nursi would say that, while one enjoys the art and beauty of the universe, it is important to remember its Sustainer. To be in awe of the individual aspects of the universe's art and beauty without remembering the Creator behind them is a mistake. Thus, says Nursi, when believers look at flowers, they should not be satisfied with saying simply "how beautiful they are." Instead, a believer should say "how beautifully they are made."[22]

Nursi specifies that creatures should be loved because of being created by God. He notes that love in one's heart is a reflection of God and belongs to Him. Love for ephemeral things should not occupy one's heart. Such love will lead to grief and sadness. On the other hand, if one loves creatures because of God, then they will bring genuine love and happiness.

Nursi further elaborates his point with an example of an apple. Imagine receiving an apple from a mighty king, he suggests. In this apple, there are two types of love and taste. The first kind of love is the love you have for this gift because it is an apple; you love the apple because of itself. In this case, your love is not related to the one who gave the apple to you. Desire and satisfaction are at the center of such love. The king may not be pleased with such reaction. Your enjoyment of the apple remains until you eat it.

19. Nursi, *Words*, 301.
20. Nursi, *Mesnevî-i Nuriye*, 72.
21. Nursi, *Mesnevî-i Nuriye*, 72.
22. Nursi, *Sözler*, 873.

Because the enjoyment ends with consumption, there is also disappoint-ment.[23] The second kind of love is related to the meaning of having received an apple from a mighty and compassionate king. Receiving an apple from the king is a great boon. In accepting the apple, one shows appreciation of such a gift. From such a perspective, the taste of such an apple is a thou-sandfold better than the taste of any other apple; this is thankfulness and respect. As in this example, Nursi concludes:

> In exactly the same way, if all bounties and fruits are loved for themselves, if they are thoughtlessly delighted in only for the material pleasures that they yield, that love is merely love of self. Also, those pleasures are transient and bring pain. But, if they are loved as favours proceeding from Almighty God's mercy and as fruits of His munificence, and if pleasure is obtained from them with good appetite by appreciating the degree of kindness in that munificence and favour, then it has both the meaning of gratitude and is a pain-free pleasure.[24]

In Nursi's perspective, there is no room for nihilism and despair. Strong faith with right perspective is the most important element of shattering the states of nihilism and despair. It brings the windows of beauty. With a strong faith, Nursi sees beauty even in evil and suffering. To sum up, es-tablishing a positive outlook in one's mind liberates the person from falling into a destructive attitude. Once the inner world is freed from a pessimistic worldview, the individual attains strength in overcoming hardships. The re-sponse to suffering is a constructive one. If God is in charge of the universe, beauty and wisdom overrule all apparent evil. A human being can then interpret events around the world in optimistic ways, maintain hope, and engage with challenges through persistent active service.

Seeing Beauty Even in Suffering

As discussed in chapter 1, Nursi witnessed the collapse of the Ottoman Empire and the colonization of the Muslim world. Nursi's life span coin-cided with the two most destructive wars in history: World War I and II. He spent most of his life in exile and prison. Many of his followers were impris-oned as well. In the *Risale*, Nursi naturally reflected on the individual and

23. Nursi, *Sözler*, 873.
24. Nursi, *Words*, 671.

communal sufferings and tribulations of people. In his reflections, Nursi draws the attention of his readers to a beautiful aspect of suffering and evil.

In contextualizing suffering and trials, Nursi frequently emphasized an important characteristic of Islamic theology, which is embodied in this qur'anic verse: "He has the keys to the unseen: no one knows them but Him. He knows all that is in the land and sea. No leaf falls without His knowledge, nor is there a single grain in the darkness of the earth or anything, fresh or withered, that is not written in a clear Record."[25] Accordingly, nothing lies outside God's knowledge. Everything belongs to God, which is a point made in the Qur'an.[26] Therefore, God "does what He wills."[27]

In various places of his *Risale*, Nursi attempts to answer whether suffering and God's compassion are compatible. In order to address this complex theological question, Nursi turns to God's Ninety-Nine Beautiful Names (*asma al-husna*), a recurring theme in Islamic theology. This world and the human being as microcosmos are limited (but unique) configurations and manifestations of these divine names.

For example, to explain why God allows suffering, Nursi constructs an elaborate analogy featuring a fashion designer and a model. Once the model is hired, Nursi states, s/he does not have the right to complain because of the dresses that would be tried on him/her. The designer has the right to try various versions of the dress on the model. In this case, s/he does not have the right to say "I do not want this dress." Nursi then asks us to imagine that there is a beautiful designer dress, which is very much liked by that fashion model. All of a sudden, the designer decides to change the dress. In this situation, the model does not have the right to say "Do not change this dress, because I like it so much."[28] Likewise, Nursi asserts, each single creature should be considered as God's fashion model. Without changes in creatures—such as sickness, death, or various types of suffering—there is no way for people to know God.[29] It is through these alterations that one becomes acquainted with God's attributes, which are embodied in creation. For instance, one of God's names is *al-shafi'*, the one who heals. If there is

---

25. Qur'an 6:59.
26. Qur'an 42:53.
27. Qur'an 14:27.
28. Nursi, *Mektubat*, 271.
29. Nursi, *Mektubat*, 272.

no illness, there is no way to discern that God is the Healer—a necessary step toward deep experiential knowledge of God.[30]

Healing is closely related to mercy and compassion. Through illness, Nursi explains, one may come to know God as *al-rahim* (the Giver of Mercy) or as *al-qadir* (the Almighty). One of God's names is *al-muhyi*, the Giver of Life. But "life" requires death—out of which new life may come. That spring brings new life following death brought by winter is a good illustration of this. Life and death are mirror images of God's Names equally, because each represents a different aspect of God's creative process.

God is also *al-karim* (the Most Generous) and *al-razzaq* (the Provider), Nursi reminds us. These Names of God "require" the existence of the needy.[31] That is, that God is Generous and All-Providing has no meaning unless there be creatures who call upon God to meet their needs. Without someone to ask for something of him, to call a very generous person *al-karim* is meaningless.

Just as any beautiful person likes his or her beauty to be seen, says Nursi,[32] so God loves to reveal His beauty and perfection through the Ninety-Nine Names; but that revealing sometimes necessitates suffering. A *hadith al-qudsi*[33] foundational to Nursi's theology of suffering goes like this:

> God the Exalted will say on the Day of Resurrection: O son of Adam, I was sick but you did not visit me. He will say: O my Lord, how can I visit you when you are the Lord of the worlds? God will say: Did you not know that my servant was sick and you did not visit him, and had you visited him you would have found me with him? O son of Adam, I asked you for food but you did not feed me. He will say: My Lord, how can I feed you when you are the Lord of the worlds? God will say: Did you not know that my servant asked you for food but you did not feed him, and had you fed him you would have found me with him? O son of Adam, I asked you for drink but you did not provide for me. He will say: My Lord, how can I give you drink when you are the Lord of the worlds? God will say: My servant asked you for a drink but you did not provide for him, and had you given it to him you would have found me with him.[34]

30. Nursi, *Lem'alar*, 216.

31. Nursi, *Lem'alar*, 216.

32. Nursi, *Mektubat*, 275.

33. A *hadith al-qudsi* is a sacred narration; from the perspective of its meaning, it is from God, but from the perspective of its words, it is from the Prophet Muhammad.

34. "Sahih Muslim," https://sunnah.com/muslim/45/54.

This *hadith* stresses that suffering is a trial for the one who suffers and the person who can help. It teaches that God is involved in the process. It presents a vivid picture of God as present in human suffering.

Nursi's point—made as one who suffered enormously throughout his adult life—is that all facets of suffering indeed have beautiful dimensions.[35] It is through suffering, he asserts, that human beings can progress, that they can move toward perfection. Without upsets, turbulence, or illnesses, life is static and monotonous.[36] Suffering motivates people to evolve—morally, spiritually, and intellectually. Nursi asserts that this should come as no surprise. After all, Islamic theology teaches that suffering may bring one closer to God, drawing considerable attention to the suffering of the prophets, including the suffering of Prophet Muhammad himself, to make this point.[37] Nursi insists however that the progress occasioned by suffering is also material. From his point of view, without trials and tribulations, it would be difficult to imagine people's progress, for instance, in human rights and medicine. It is because of ongoing suffering that the progress of human beings remains unceasing. Suffering also strengthens virtues such as patience and humility. From Nursi's point of view, without struggles and trials, "being patient" has no meaning. Illnesses make people aware of their impotence; thus, they become willing to seek refuge in God and to find strength there. Unless we suffer, Nursi points out, we are unlikely to appreciate what we have or what is beautiful.[38] Without sickness, he believes, we are unlikely to value health properly. Without hunger, we may not be able to appreciate wealth. Without death, it is difficult to understand the importance of life.[39]

Death as a Blessing and Manifestation to Know God

Nursi saw beauty not only in suffering, but also in death. Seeing the beautiful aspects of death, he instructs his readers, is part of the process of forming a positive mind and heart. As the *Risale* makes clear in its reflections on manifestations of God's Names, one of those names is *al-mumit*, the one who causes death. Thus, as Nursi often points out in his writings, death is

35. Nursi, *Sözler*, 702.
36. Nursi, *Lem'alar*, 10.
37. Qur'an 46:35.
38. Nursi, *Şu'alar*, 27–28.
39. Nursi, *Mektubat*, 273.

a means to know God. Like life, death is also a gift of God.[40] While life is a sign of God's oneness, says Nursi, death is a sign of His unity: "Just as life, which displays a manifestation of Divine beauty, is a proof of Divine oneness, and a sort of manifestation of unity, death too, which displays the manifestation of Divine glory, is a proof of Divine unity."[41] Nursi then utilizes an analogy of the sun and the bubbles in order to expand on his point:

> For example, *And God's is the highest similitude*, by showing the sun's light and reflection, the bubbles on a wide flowing river which sparkle in the sun and transparent objects which glisten on the face of the earth testify to the sun. On those tribes of bubbles and transparent objects disappearing, the continued magnificent manifestation of the sun and the uninterrupted and constant display of its light on the successive groups and tribes of bubbles and transparent objects which follow on after them, testify decisively that the little images of the sun and the lights and flashes which appear and sparkle, flare up and die away, and are changed and renewed, are the manifestations of an enduring, perpetual, elevated, single Sun whose manifestation is undying. That is to say, just as through their appearance and becoming visible, the shining droplets demonstrate the sun's existence, so with their disappearance and extinction, they demonstrate its continuation, permanence, and unity.[42]

According to Nursi's analogy, the disappearance and reappearance of the bubbles on the surface of the river is a sign of the continuity of the sun. In relation to God and deaths in the universe, the implication of Nursi's analogy is this:

> In exactly the same way, through their existence and lives these flowing beings testify to the necessary existence and oneness of the Necessarily Existent One, and with their deaths and disappearance, they testify to His pre-eternity, everlastingness, and unity. Yes, the beautiful creatures and fine beings which are renewed and restored within the decline and disappearance that occur through the alternation of night and day, winter and summer, and the centuries and ages, surely point to the existence, continuance, and unity of an elevated, eternal possessor of continually manifested beauty. While the deaths and disappearance of those beings

40. Nursi, *Letters*, 24.

41. Nursi, *Words*, 312.

42. Nursi, *Words*, 312.

together with their apparent and lowly causes demonstrate that the causes are nothing but a mere veil. This situation proves decisively that these arts, these inscriptions, these manifestations, are the constantly renewed arts, the changing inscriptions, the moving mirrors of an All-Beauteous One of Glory, all of Whose Names are sacred and beautiful; that they are His seals which follow on one after the other, and His stamps that are changed with wisdom.[43]

Here, for Nursi, the constant changes, disappearances and reappearances, deaths, and circulations are the manifestations of God's Names and windows into knowing Him.

On another occasion, Nursi attempts to show life and beauty in death by pointing to seeds as examples. He explains that, while it appears that a seed dies and disintegrates, in reality it yields life. Likewise, the death of human beings should not be regarded as destruction or an end, but rather as "the sign, introduction, and starting point of perpetual life."[44]

Nursi further asserts that one way to know God is through the opposites in the universe. He points out that, with the mirror of darkness, we can understand the degree of the intensity of light. Likewise, as he affirms, "beings act as mirrors to the Maker's power through their impotence and to His riches through their poverty; similarly, they act as mirrors to His everlastingness through their ephemerality."[45] Nursi then raises a thought-provoking question, which might be in the minds of many in our time: How can death be regarded as a blessing? Reflecting on the qur'anic verse 67:2: "[He] who created death and life to test you and reveal which of you does best," Nursi argues that like life, death is a blessing. He points to some of the aspects of death as blessing, which are worth quoting at length:

> The First: Death is a great bounty because it means one is freed from the duties and obligations of life, which become burdensome. It is also a door through which one passes in order to join and be united with one's friends, ninety-nine out of a hundred of whom are already in the Intermediate Realm.
>
> The Second: It is to be released from the narrow, irksome, turbulent prison of this world, and to receive an expansive, joyful, troublefree immortal life, and to enter the sphere of the Eternally Beloved One's mercy.

43. Nursi, *Words*, 313.
44. Nursi, *Letters*, 284.
45. Nursi, *Letters*, 286.

The Third: There are numerous factors like old age, which make life arduous and show death to be a far superior bounty. For example, if together with your very elderly parents who cause you much distress you beheld before you your grandfather's grandfathers in all their pitiful state, you would understand what a calamity life is, and what a bounty, death. Another example: one can imagine how difficult life is in the harsh conditions of winter for the beautiful flying insects, the lovers of the beautiful flowers, and what a mercy death is for them.

The Fourth: Just as sleep is a comfort, a mercy, a rest, particularly for those afflicted by disaster and the wounded and the sick, so too is death, the elder brother of sleep, a pure bounty and mercy for the disaster-struck and those who suffer tribulations that drive them to suicide.[46]

Here, Nursi is straightforward. In the face of the tendency to regard death as destruction, he wishes to demonstrate that, in many ways, death is a beautiful blessing. Needless to say, Nursi makes these assertions on the premise that his reader has embraced faith in God and the hereafter. However, because he provides examples from nature, even people of no faith may be able to relate to his writings. From his point of view, imagining a world without death is more burdensome than comforting. To care forever for elderly parents would certainly present a challenge. Endless suffering would also be unbearable. Death, as Nursi stresses, surely is more favorable.

That the exact time of death remains hidden is also considered a blessing by Nursi. If its moment of occurrence were known, people would spend the first half of their life in heedlessness; yet, for the second half, they would be in constant terror, knowing that the time of their end was drawing near. On the other hand, death's hiddenness leaves people in a state between hope and fear. Furthermore, if the time of one's death were known, then the idea of being tested in this world would be undermined. Nursi then concludes that, because of death's unpredictability, "Everyone therefore continually bears in mind both his death and his continued life, and he works both for this world and the hereafter. He is also aware that the end of the world may occur in any age, or that it may continue, and so works for eternal life within the transitory nature of this world, and strives to build the world as though he was never going to die."[47] Having presented death as a beautiful

46. Nursi, *Letters*, 24–25.
47. Nursi, *Rays*, 100.

blessing and manifestation to know God, in what follows, our focus is how Nursi derives hope and life from death.

Seeing Hope and Life in Death

In various places in his *Risale*, Nursi points out that death is not destruction or annihilation; rather, it is a transition to new life. To his mind, a believer should not be in a state of despair and pessimism when reflecting upon death's reality. Death is to be regarded simply as a discharge from assigned duties.

One day, during the month of Ramadan, Nursi visited the Bayezid Mosque in Istanbul and listened to a recitation of the Qur'an that included this verse from the Qur'an: "Every soul is certain to taste death."[48] The message of this verse occupied his world: "It entered my ear, penetrated to the depths of my heart and established itself there; it shattered my profound sleep and heedlessness. I went out of the mosque. Because of the stupor of the sleep which for a long time had settled in my head, for several days a tempest raged in it."[49]

Further meditation on the verse uncovered other meanings for Nursi: "The human race is a living creature; it shall die in order to be resurrected. The globe of the earth is a living creature; it also will die in order to take on an eternal form. The world too is a living creature; it will die in order to assume the form of the hereafter."[50] In turn, this led him to meditate on his own situation:

> While in this state, I considered my situation. I saw that youth, which is the source of pleasure, was departing; while old age, the source of sorrow, was approaching; that life, which is so shining and luminous, was taking its leave; while death, which is terrifying and apparently darkness, was preparing to arrive; and that the lovable world, which is thought to be permanent and is the beloved of the heedless, was hastening to its decease.[51]

48. Qur'an 3:185.
49. Nursi, *Flashes*, 296.
50. Nursi, *Flashes*, 297.
51. Nursi, *Flashes*, 297.

In the midst of such despair, Nursi heard another Qur'an verse from the reciter: "And give the good news to those who believe."[52] This verse's message became a remedy for him—offering him great hope, uncovering light from darkness. For Nursi, the qur'anic message dismantles the horror of death: "With its effulgence, I sought consolation, hope, and light, within the points at which I had felt horror, desolation and despair, not outside them. Endless thanks be to Almighty God, I found the cure within the malady itself, I found the light within the darkness itself, I found the solace within the horror itself."[53]

From the verse, Nursi draws fresh perspective on death:

> Death is not annihilation and separation, but the introduction to eternal life, its beginning. It is a rest from the hardships of life's duties, a demobilization. It is a change of residence. It is to meet with the caravan of one's friends who have already migrated to the Intermediate World; and so on. I saw death's true, beautiful face through truths like these. I looked at death's face not with fear, but with a sort of longing. I understood one meaning of the Sufis' contemplation of death.[54]

Darkness, pessimism, and despair regarding death fade away. Death brings hope and life now. In fact, at this point, it is perceived as beautiful and desirable for him. In another place, Nursi remarks that, with the help of faith in God, he began to love death.[55] However, he still raises the point that since, in the end, blessings face death, it is difficult to enjoy them completely. Seeing the end dismantles the pleasure.

Nursi then offers another insight. While creatures face physical death in one aspect, in many others they fulfill their duties, however. As an example, Nursi offers a rose: It flourishes, fades, and then dies. While the rose has died, it yet remains in people's minds. It becomes somewhat eternalized. In addition, the rose's forms and meanings are continued by its successor blossoms.[56] Analogously, he notes, once a word is out of a person's mouth, it seems lost. But its myriad forms and meanings last in the ears, on paper,

---

52. Qur'an 2:225.
53. Nursi, *Flashes*, 297.
54. Nursi, *Flashes*, 298.
55. Nursi, *Rays*, 25.
56. Nursi, *Mesnevî-i Nuriye*, 63.

in books, and in minds. As with the rose, an apparent death yields lives in different forms.[57]

Remembering Death as a Means for Detachment

In his *Letters to an American Lady*, C. S. Lewis, a contemporary of Nursi, writes: "There are, aren't there, only three things we can do about death: to desire it, to fear it, or to ignore it."[58] For Lewis, a true believer would desire death. While Nursi would wholeheartedly agree with Lewis, he also focused on the benefits of remembering death, which has been an important aspect of Islamic spirituality.

Nursi believed that once people had contemplated the reality that everything but God is subject to departure and death, they would not attach their hearts to ephemeral things. In fact, in a letter to one of his students, Nursi refers to a plaque hanging above his bed, on which was a statement about death: "If you want advice, death is sufficient. Yes, the person who thinks of death is saved from love of this world, and works in earnest for the hereafter."[59]

Nursi then reflects on the qur'anic story of the Prophet Joseph, which the Qur'an calls "the best of stories."[60] At the end of the story, Joseph asks God to make him die in righteousness.[61] The fact that the most beautiful story would conclude with mentioning death astonishes Nursi. He points out that, when a happy story ends with a reminder of death and separation, it dismantles the readers' joy and makes the story more painful for them—and in the qur'anic account, death is mentioned when Joseph is at the peak of happiness and joy. Having been betrayed by his brothers and sold into slavery, he had risen to an important rank and, in the end, was reunited with his family. The fact that Joseph asks God for his death demonstrates his belief that there is a greater happiness beyond death. According to Nursi, this is why the end of the story does not cause any sorrow to those who listen to it; rather, it "gives good tidings and adds further joy."[62]

---

57. Nursi, *Mesnevî-i Nuriye*, 63.
58. Lewis, *Letters to an American Lady*, 84.
59. Nursi, *Letters*, 334.
60. Qur'an 12:3.
61. Qur'an 12:101.
62. Nursi, *Letters*, 335.

Remembering death, Nursi insists, prevents people from being heedless and attached to the things of this world.[63]

Nursi reads the story of the Prophet Abraham in the Qur'an in a similar fashion. In the story, Abraham is searching for his Lord.[64] When the night falls, Abraham sees a star and says, "This is my Lord." But when the star sets, he says, "I do not love things that set." Abraham then sees the moon and says, "This is my Lord"; but when it too disappears, he realizes that it cannot be his Lord either. Upon seeing the sunrise and sunset, he uses the same reasoning. Abraham's search results in this conclusion: "I have turned my face as a true believer towards Him who created the heavens and the earth. I am not one of the polytheists."[65] Nursi contemplates the story of Abraham at great length. The gist of his insight is that the heart cannot be attached to those things that are subject to death and departure. When people are attached to such things, they cannot help but be disappointed. Loving the things that are subject to death is not worthwhile, says Nursi, because things that are subject to death are not, in reality, beautiful. A heart that is created to be the mirror of the love of God, to love things that are eternal, precludes love of ephemeral things.[66]

Remembering Death as a Means of Forming a Virtuous Character

Although it has become a less common practice in this modern era, building a virtuous character through the remembrance of death has long been part of religious traditions. For example, the Latin phrase *memento mori* (remember that you must die) was a mantra in medieval Christianity—an important practice in building a good character. Such a practice has equally been important in the Islamic tradition. The *hadith* collections usually include a book of *jana'iz*, a section devoted to the subject of death. The Sufi tradition takes remembering death as a significant element of its spirituality and formation of a virtuous character. The last—and longest—book of Al-Ghazali's *Ihyā' 'Ulūm al-Dīn* is about death and the hereafter.

Remembering death as a means toward formation of a virtuous character also appears in the *Risale*. We shall offer a few examples. First, Nursi

63. Nursi, *Letters*, 335.

64. For the related story, see Qur'an 6:74–79.

65. Qur'an 6:79.

66. Nursi, *Words*, 228.

believed that remembering death is an important means to attain sincerity. He notes that pretentiousness and excessive attachment to worldly benefits are the obstacles to sincerity. Remembering death will keep believers from pretentiousness and will protect them from the tricks of their egos. That is why qur'anic verses such as "every soul shall taste death"[67] and "truly you will die one day, and truly they too will die one day"[68] were crucial for Sufis and all people of truth. They made the contemplation of death central to their spiritual life.[69] Nursi stresses that the Sufis "imagined themselves to be dead and being placed in the grave. With prolonged thought the evil-commanding soul becomes saddened and affected by such imagining and gives up its far-reaching ambitions and hopes to an extent."[70] Nursi offers a slightly different method for his followers in remembering death:

> Since our way is not that of the Sufis but of reality, we are not compelled to perform this contemplation in an imaginary and hypothetical form like they do. To do so is anyway not in conformity with the way of reality. Our way is not to bring the future to the present by thinking of the end, but to travel in the mind to the future from the present in respect of reality, and to gaze on it. Yes, dispensing with the need to imagine, one may look on one's own corpse, the single fruit on the tree of this brief life. One may look on one's own death, and if one goes a bit further, see the death of this century, and going further still, observe the death of this world, opening up the way to complete sincerity.[71]

Here, Nursi proposes a way of contemplating death that will not interrupt worldly affairs. Constantly remembering death and thinking one's own death will bring the faithful to an ideal state of sincerity. In fact, it leads to a joyful life—a life without feeling remorse or regret at the end but to appreciate it to its fullest.

Nursi also believes that thinking about death will make people humbler and more sensitive to their fellow human beings. In fact, his students remarked that, during World War II, Nursi was very concerned about the destructive side of wars. He invited those involved in wars to think about the ephemera of this world, to think about mortality, and thus to

67. Qur'an 3:185.

68. Qur'an 39:30.

69. Nursi, *Flashes*, 217.

70. Nursi, *Flashes*, 217.

71. Nursi, *Flashes*, 217.

understand why enmity should be left behind.[72] Here, Nursi's approach is similar to that expressed by Ernest Becker in his book *The Denial of Death*. Becker attempts to show that there is a direct correlation between *not* facing our mortality and the fostering of conflict. As did Nursi before him, Becker asserts that facing our mortality will make our world a better place.[73]

In Nursi's writings, his discussion of death often occurs in the context of discussion of jealousy and enmity. Nursi regarded these emotions as potentially destructive. To people occupied with jealousy, which leads to enmity, Nursi recommends thinking about the ephemeral nature of the objects of that jealousy. To a person whose heart is full of enmity and jealousy toward a rival because of the worldly skills and blessings that rival has, Nursi counsels recollection that "the beauty, strength, rank, and wealth possessed by his rival are transient and temporary."[74] They may be beautiful, but they also bring burden.[75]

As a further step of building positive minds and hearts, Nursi points to impotence (*acz*), poverty (*fakr*), compassion (*şefkat*), and contemplation (*tefekkür*) as the elements of his inward *jihad* on the journey of the spiritual path. This is the subject of our next chapter.

72. Nursi, *Barla Lahikası*, 38.
73. See Becker, *Denial of Death*.
74. Nursi, *Letters*, 315.
75. Nursi, *Letters*, 315.

Chapter 5

Elements of Inward *Jihad*

THE ETHIC OF NONVIOLENT positive action modeled and taught by Nursi presumes a willingness to travel a Godward path. All Islamic spiritual paths, Nursi acknowledges, are founded on the Qur'an. However, some are more efficient than others. The path he commends to his followers, as he himself explains, is short, convenient, and direct: "follow the practices (*sunna*) of the Prophet Muhammad, perform the religious obligations and give up serious sins. And it is especially to perform the prescribed prayers correctly and with attention, and following them to say the *tesbihat* or invocations."[1] Simple as it is, this path does have elements to be cultivated and four steps (*hatves*) to internalize them. In various parts of the *Risale*, Nursi identifies these elements of inward *jihad* as impotence (*acz*), poverty (*fakr*), compassion (*şefkat*), and contemplation (*tefekkür*)—each of which shall be explained in the following.[2]

Impotence (*acz*): Finding Power in Powerlessness

For Nursi, impotence (*acz*) is one of the most significant aspects of being human on the Godward path, as critical as love. Thus, part of the mission of the *Risale* is to make human beings aware of their weakness, as being aware of one's weakness is an essential step toward surrender and toward becoming a servant of God—who is, of course, beyond all weakness.[3] Recognition

1. Nursi, *Words*, 491.
2. Nursi, *Words*, 491.
3. Nursi, *Words*, 491.

of human impotence is thus a fundamental means by which the believer is led to explore God's attributes—to come to know God as Almighty, the most Merciful and the most Generous.[4] Without powerlessness, God remains unknown to human beings.

Nursi draws an analogy to the sun in order to elucidate his point that exploring one's weakness may lead to a closer relationship with God. Things that reflect the light of the sun are those that turn their face toward it. The reflection, however, is never as strong as the sun's direct light. Similarly, people may be mirrors of God's attributes, but they must be aware of their limits in relation to God. Awareness of these polar opposites—the unlimited weakness of human beings and the unlimited power of God—provides insight into God's power, richness, and glory.[5]

Nursi notes that with old age comes weakness, or impotence. But, he suggests, the elderly need not be very much concerned about this situation, because "the weakness and powerlessness of old age are means for attracting divine grace and mercy."[6] Pointing toward his own personal experience, Nursi asserts that, during the challenges and weaknesses in his life, God bestowed His mercy and compassion on him.[7] Pointing to animals as an example, he notes:

> For the weakest and most powerless of animals are the young. But then it is they who receive the sweetest and most beautiful manifestation of mercy. The powerlessness of a young bird in the nest at the top of a tree attracts the manifestation of mercy to employ its mother like an obedient soldier. Its mother flies all around and brings it its food. When with its wings growing strong the nestling forgets its impotence, its mother tells it to go and find its own food, and no longer listens to it.[8]

Just as do the young of the animal world, Nursi insists, elderly human beings will receive divine mercy and compassion in their weakness and

4. Nursi, *Lem'alar*, 546.

5. Nursi, *Mesnevî-i Nuriye*, 152.

6. Nursi, *Flashes*, 302.

7. Nursi mentions, for example, his time as a hostage in Russia. He remarks that, although he was old and did not speak any Russian, he was able to escape. Because of his weakness and impotence, with God's blessing, Nursi points out, he traveled a distance that would take a year on foot. Through Warshova and Austria, he came to Istanbul. See Nursi, *Flashes*, 300.

8. Nursi, *Flashes*, 302.

powerlessness.[9] In Nursi's interpretation, acknowledging one's weakness in relation to God's power is a major asset for the journey of the spiritual *jihad*.

Poverty (*fakr*)

As Nursi uses the term, poverty (*fakr*)—the second element of the path of spiritual *jihad*—is a comprehensive concept. It refers to the aspect of human beings that they are extremely dependent and in need.[10] Being aware of this disposition brings one closer to God. Without the unlimited poverty of human beings, one cannot understand the unlimited richness of God.[11] Nursi explains that the way the darkness of the night reveals a light, in the same way human beings' poverty and need, their defects and faults, "make[s] known the power, strength, richness, and mercy of an All-Powerful One of Glory."[12] He also states that "utter poverty and endless need" of human beings leads them to seek for a point of assistance in the face of their innumerable aims. This point of assistance is no one but God, who can fulfill all of their needs.[13]

Compassion (*şefkat*)

The third element in Nursi's understanding of inner *jihad* is compassion. In fact, it is his path's essence, as central as love to the Godward path. As the *Risale* makes clear,[14] showing mercy is important, but the way of compassion is, Nursi says, even more effective and comprehensive.

In order to further his point, Nursi undertakes a comparison of the concepts of love and compassion. According to the Qur'an, he says, compassion is the higher virtue: the Qur'an presents the Prophet Jacob's compassion for his son with more favorability than Zulaikha's love for the Prophet Joseph. Going a step farther, he suggests that one's compassion for one's own child brings forth one's compassion for other children—even for

9. Nursi, *Flashes*, 302.
10. Nursi, *Words*, 491.
11. Nursi, *Lem'alar*, 39.
12. Nursi, *Words*, 719.
13. Nursi, *Words*, 719.
14. Nursi, *Lem'alar*, 325.

all creatures that have life. It has no expectation. Even the sacrifice and care of ordinary animals for their babies are good examples for such compassion. There is sincerity in compassion.[15]

The path of compassion is related to God's name *al-rahim* (the most Compassionate). Those who embody compassion become mirrors of this divine name.[16] Love, however, is more limited. A person who is in love with someone looks at everything from the beloved's perspective and may sacrifice everything for their sake. In order to elevate the status of the beloved, the lover lowers the status of others and denounces them.[17] To further emphasize his point, Nursi refers to a poem in which a lover says, "the sun is hiding because of the beauty of my beloved, it is shy of her beauty; that is why she is wearing the veil of cloud." From Nursi's perspective, it is not fair that the lover interprets the sun in this regard because it is the manifestation of God's light.[18]

Compassion—the essence of his *Risale*—was Nursi's rule of life for more than thirty years. Not only would he never harm those who unjustly tortured and imprisoned him, but he never cursed them. From Nursi's perspective, any harm visited on his oppressor—even cursing—might harm innocent people under the care of those oppressors, such as their elderly parents and children. For the sake of such innocent people, Nursi avoided harming his oppressors, and even forgave them.[19]

Because of the principle of compassion, Nursi advised his students to refrain from involvement in anything that would violate the public order. Nursi comments that some of the members of law enforcement even admitted that "the students of the *Risale* are like spiritual police, they keep the public in order."[20] The attitude and behavior of his students for twenty years are a great testimony in this regard: in the law enforcement record, not even one case of public disorder being caused by any of the thousands of students of the *Risale* can be found.[21]

15. Nursi, *Lem'alar*, 325.

16. Nursi, *Sözler*, 641.

17. Nursi, *Mektubat*, 57.

18. Nursi, *Letters*, 49.

19. Nursi, *Emirdağ Lahikası I*, 354.

20. Nursi, *Emirdağ Lahikası I*, 562.

21. Nursi, *Emirdağ Lahikası I*, 562. For more on Nursi's notion of avoidance of political involvement and its relation to his understanding of compassion, see chapter 7.

For Nursi, the personal consequence of excessive compassion toward his fellow human beings took the form of feeling much older than his biological age. Nursi's concern extended to the sufferings of the global community.[22] His reflections on the sufferings of people during World War II exemplify this. He mentions that he was deeply saddened, particularly by the death of innocent women, elderly, and children killed during the war. When confrontation with so much suffering, sadness, and despair becomes overwhelming, faith comes as a savior: "Suddenly I felt in my heart, those innocent people killed during the war, would be considered martyrs and elevated to the status of saints. Their temporary lives would turn into an eternal one. Their properties that were lost or looted during the war would be considered as charity and turn into an eternal property."[23]

Nursi continues, saying that "even if these innocent people are disbelievers, God will reward them from His treasure because of their sufferings in this world. I came to believe without any doubt that if the veil of unseen would be uncovered the situation of these innocent people, they would say 'O God, thanks to be our God.'"[24]

Nursi's compassion was not limited to his fellow beings, but also animals and plants. Here, it is worth citing Nursi's feelings in this regard in a lengthy quotation:

> One time when observing the season of spring, I saw that the successive caravans of beings, and especially living creatures and the small young ones at that, which followed on one after the other and in a flowing torrent displaying hundreds of thousands of samples of the resurrection of the dead and Great Gathering on the face of the earth, appeared only briefly then disappeared. The tableaux of death and transience amid that constant, awesome activity seemed to me excessively sad; I felt such pity it made me weep. The more I observed the deaths of those lovely small creatures, the more my heart ached. I cried at the pity of it and within me felt a deep spiritual turmoil. Life which met with such an end seemed to me to be torment worse than death.
>
> The living beings of the plant and animal kingdoms, too, which were most beautiful and lovable and full of valuable art, opened their eyes for a moment onto the exhibition of the universe, then disappeared and were gone. I felt grievous pain the

22. Nursi, *Lem'alar*, 396.

23. Nursi, *Kastamonu Lahikası*, 97.

24. Nursi, *Kastamonu Lahikası*, 97.

more I watched this. My heart wanted to weep and complain and cry out at fate. It asked the awesome questions: "Why do they come and then depart without stopping?" These apparently useless, purposeless little creatures were being dispatched to non-existence before my very eyes, despite having been created, nurtured and raised with so much attention and art, in such valuable form. They were merely torn up like rags and thrown away into the obscurity of nothingness. The more I saw this the more my inner senses and faculties, which are captivated by beauty and perfection and enamoured of precious things, cried out: "Why does no one take pity on them? Isn't it a shame? Where did they come from, the death and ephemerality in these bewildering upheavals and transformations which persistently attack these wretched beings?"[25]

In this situation of sadness resulting from his compassion toward the entirety of creation, Nursi finds remedy in the Qur'an and his faith (*iman*). He then explores the wisdom of such transformation:

All living beings, for instance this adorned flower or that sweet-producing bee, are Divine odes full of meaning which innumerable conscious beings study in delight. They are precious miracles of power and proclamations of wisdom exhibiting their Maker's art in captivating fashion to innumerable appreciative observers. While to appear before the gaze of the Glorious Creator, Who wishes to observe His art Himself, and look on the beauties of His creation and the loveliness of the manifestations of His Names, is another exceedingly elevated result of their creation.[26]

Here, Nursi sees a hand of wisdom behind the transformation and the departure of creatures.

Some of the testimonies of Nursi's students about his compassion toward animals might be helpful to further understand his attitude. Molla Hamid Ekinci recalls that, one day during the summer he spent with Nursi on the mountain Erek near the city of Van, Nursi had told his students that they could wander on the mountain while he secluded himself for a period of supplication-making. Off went the students. Later, as he and his students made their way back to the village, Nursi asked them what they had done during their free time. Molla Hamid told him that he had seen a lizard on a rock and had killed it. Nursi was very saddened by that report and told Molla Hamid that he committed a grievous mistake. Molla Hamid

25. Nursi, *Rays*, 21–22.
26. Nursi, *Rays*, 21–22.

countered that he had heard that killing a lizard garnered as much reward as performing *hajj* (pilgrimage). Nursi then sat the students down for a serious lesson on ethics:

> Nursi asked: "Did the lizard attack you?"
>
> Molla Hamid: "No, it did not."
>
> Nursi: "Did it grab anything from you?"
>
> Molla Hamid: "No, it did not."
>
> Nursi: "Did it occupy your own land?"
>
> Molla Hamid: "No, it did not."
>
> Nursi: "Are you the one who provides food for this animal?"
>
> Molla Hamid: "No, I am not."
>
> Nursi: "Did you create this animal?"
>
> Molla Hamid: "No, I did not."
>
> Nursi: "Do you know the purpose and wisdom behind the creation of these animals?"
>
> Molla Hamid: "No, I do not know."
>
> Nursi: "Did God create this animal so that you kill it?"
>
> Molla Hamid: "No, I do not think so."
>
> Nursi: "Then who told you to kill this animal? The wisdom behind the creation of such animals is boundless. Indeed, you committed a grave mistake."[27]

As evident, Nursi's approach of compassion does not leave any room for violence against fellow human beings, or other creatures in the universe.

Contemplation (*tefekkür*)

The fourth element of Nursi's spiritual *jihad* is contemplation (*tefekkür*). Nursi points out that contemplation, like love—but even more enriching, more shining, and more comprehensive—is a way that leads to God.[28] It is a great step in understanding God's attribute *al-hakim* (the Wise).[29] In

---

27. Akgündüz, *Arşiv Belgeleri Işığında*, 518.

28. Nursi remarks that he basically expands the practice of *muraqaba* (meditation) in Sufism by adding the practice of *tefekkür* (contemplation) to it. See Nursi, *Bediüzzaman'ın Tarihçe-i Hayatı*, 33.

29. Nursi, *Sözler*, 641.

addition, he points out that one of the most important duties of human beings is contemplating about the letters of the universe and thinking of them.[30]

Contemplation of the universe is a major theme of the Qur'an, which repeatedly draws the attention of the believers to the beauties of the universe. One of the most recurring words in the Qur'an is *aya* ("sign"; pl. *ayat*). As the verses of the Qur'an are referred to as *ayat*, likewise the creation is also called *ayat*. The Qur'an repeatedly invites believers to contemplate the creation: "There truly are signs in the creation of the heavens and earth, and in the alternation of night and day, for those with understanding, who remember God standing, sitting, and lying down, who reflect on the creation of the heavens and earth: 'Our Lord! You have not created all this without purpose—You are far above that!—so protect us from the torment of the Fire."[31]

Contemplation is also an important practice of the *sunna*, or an example of the Prophet Muhammad. According to a *hadith* (or report) narrated by Muhammad's wife Aisha, a pair of visitors asked her to tell them something very important about the Prophet. Aisha told them that, one night, when Muhammad got up, made *wudu* ("ablution"), and performed his prayers, she saw him weeping so much to an extent that tears were falling upon his beard and his rug had become wet. Bilal, the companion of Muhammad, came for the morning prayers. He asked Muhammad, "since all of your future and past sins are forgiven, what makes you cry?" Muhammad responded that a verse had been revealed during the previous night, and it is the message of that verse that caused him to weep: "There truly are signs in the creation of the heavens and earth, and in the alternation of night and day, for those with understanding."[32] It would be a great shame, Muhammad said, if one were to recite this verse, yet not engage in contemplation. In various places in the *Risale*, Nursi also refers to a *hadith* asserting that "an hour of contemplation (*tefekkür*) is better than one year of voluntary worship (*nafile*)."[33]

Because of the emphasis of the Qur'an and the *sunna* of Muhammad, both inward (*enfusî*) and outward (*afâkî*) contemplation are important aspects of Muslim spirituality. These practices, however, sometimes have

30. Nursi, *İlk Dönem Eserleri*, 59.

31. Qur'an 3:190–91.

32. Qur'an 3:190.

33. Nursi, *Bediüzzaman'ın Tarihçe-i Hayatı*, 574.

been overshadowed by focusing on other aspects of Islam, such as law and ritual. In his *Risale*, Nursi revives this qur'anic teaching of contemplation and makes it one of the most important aspects of his spirituality.

The universe and God's signs (*ayat*) in creation are constant themes in the Qur'an. Nursi clarifies, nevertheless, that the reason for references to the entities of the universe is not merely to describe them, but rather to draw attention to the One who creates such beauty. The Qur'an, for example, makes clear the connection between the Prophet Solomon's love for horses and the horses as signs of God when the Qur'an records him saying, "My love of fine things is part of my remembering of my Lord."[34]

Nursi repeatedly urges his disciples to study "the great book of the universe." While in the *Risale* the verses of the Qur'an provide departure points, Nursi explains them through lessons from the book of the universe. He even refers to the universe as the great Qur'an (*kur'an-ı azimi kainat*) and all creatures as miraculous verses:

> Yes, since each of the creational signs of this mighty Qur'an of the universe displays miracles to the number of points and letters of those signs, in no way could confused chance, blind force, aimless, anarchic, unconscious nature interfere in that wise, percipient particular balance and most sensitive order. If they had interfered, some traces of confusion would certainly have been apparent. Whereas no disorder of any sort is to be seen anywhere.[35]

Furthermore, Nursi signifies the universe as a place of worship (*mescit*) wherein everything worships God.[36] In this worship place, the Qur'an reads the universe. In Nursi's reading of the universe, therefore, every single creature is sacred. They are letters of God's sign. They are sacred like the pages of the written Qur'an. In the case of the Qur'an, the believers read the pages, whereas in the case of the universe, the believers testify to the signs of the creation. Reading the pages of creation in the universe and the Qur'an are thus equally important in the *Risale*.

Discussion of contemplation of the universe occupies a significant portion of Nursi's *Risale*. Perhaps the best example of his handling of this theme is his treatise entitled *The Supreme Sign* (*ayet'ül kübra*), mentioned earlier, in which a traveler observes the universe through the various

---

34. Qur'an 38:31.
35. Nursi, *Flashes*, 405.
36. Nursi, *Sözler*, 61.

aspects of creation—such as animals, rivers, mountains, plants, human beings, and more.

Contemplating the universe is also an important practice for Nursi himself. It is known that, whenever possible, he would devote significant portions of his time to wandering in nature. During his time of exile in Barla, for example, he would walk several hours to the mountain Çam Dağı, where he would spend many nights in contemplation high up in a tree. Such periods of contemplation were part of his life in other places, such as Kastamonu, Emirdağ, and Istanbul. In fact, contemplation was the motivation for his writing of the *Risale* itself.

Often contemplation becomes a relief in a state of despair and sadness. To give an example, recall that after World War I, during which he had been held captive by the Russians for almost two years, Nursi was at last able to return to Istanbul, and then to Van, where he had once taught. He found the city of Van in ruins; likewise, his former *medrese* school. He thought of his students and friends, most of whom had died in the war. This situation brought forth for him the true face of the world: it is full of sufferings. From the Qur'an comes this remedy: "Everything in the heavens and earth glorifies God—He is the Almighty, the Wise. Control of the heavens and earth belongs to Him; He gives life and death; He has power over all things."[37] Nursi says that contemplation of these verses led him to see that it was as though the fruits at the top of the fruit trees were smiling down at him, saying, "Note us as well, do not only look at the ruins." Realizing this brought to his mind the following:

> Why does an artificial letter written in the form of a town by the hand of man, who is a guest on the page of Van's plain, being wiped out by a calamitous torrent called the Russian invasion sadden you to this extent? Consider the Pre-Eternal Inscriber, everything's True Owner and Sustainer, for His missives on this page continue to be written in glittering fashion, in the way you used to see. Your weeping over those desolate ruins arises from the error of forgetting their True Owner, not thinking that men are guests and imagining them to be owner.[38]

In short, no matter how desperate the situation, contemplation of creation becomes a remedy for Nursi. It is fair to say in this regard that the universe

---

37. Qur'an 57:1–2.
38. Nursi, *Flashes*, 317.

is considered to be a cosmic community in which every single member is a manifestation of God's attributes.

Inward Contemplation

For Nursi, contemplation extends beyond the external world (*afâkî*) to the internal dimension (*enfusî*) as well. A major theme of his *Risale* is the inner state of human beings. With inward contemplation, the focus is the ego and the soul. For Nursi, "to know yourself is to know God";[39] it is also a key to understanding the universe and its creator. As he says:

> The key to the world is in the hand of man and is attached to his self. For while being apparently open, the doors of the universe are in fact closed. God Almighty has given to man by way of a Trust, such a key, called the "I", that it opens all the doors of the world; He has given him an enigmatic "I" with which he may discover the hidden treasures of the Creator of the universe. But the "I" is also an extremely complicated riddle and a talisman that is difficult to solve. When its true nature and the purpose of its creation are known, as it is itself solved, so will be the universe.[40]

Where others have regarded the self and soul as obstacles in obtaining true spirituality, Nursi sees them as means to know and understand God. The self, he explains, provides "samples and indications" of God's attributes, in order that we may know their source. The attributes embodied in the self are vehicles for exploring God's attributes.[41] In this regard, says Nursi, the self would say, for example, "as I am the owner of this house, so too is the creator the owner of the universe."[42] With regard to building the house, the self says "as I made this house and arranged it, so someone must have made the universe and arranged it."[43] Without such contemplation, Nursi believes, the true purpose of the self's creation is not known. The self may then become a dangerous tool for keeping oneself away from God, or for such misguided behavior as ascribing partners to God.[44]

---

39. For Nursi's approach to the relationship between knowing the self and God, see "Thirtieth Word" in *Words*, 150–76.

40. Nursi, *Words*, 558.

41. Nursi, *Words*, 558.

42. Nursi, *Words*, 559.

43. Nursi, *Words*, 559.

44. Nursi, *Words*, 560.

Nursi's reflections on his contemplative activities are as poetic as they are instructive. This section concludes with a sample dating from his period of exile in Barla:

> Once, when I was reflecting on Divine oneness, I looked at the fruits on the plane-tree outside my room. A chain of thought came to me as inspiration, and I write it here in Arabic exactly as it came to me.
>
> All these fruits and the seeds within them are miracles of dominical wisdom, wonders of Divine art, gifts of Divine mercy, material proofs of Divine unity, bearers of the good news that Divine favours will be granted in the hereafter. Just as they are all truthful witnesses to His all-embracing power and knowledge, each of them is a mirror confirming His unity in all the corners of the world of multiplicity and in all the parts of the world of this tree, a world that has become multiple.
>
> They turn the gaze from multiplicity to unity. Each of them says through the tongue of its being: "Do not let your glance wander over all this mighty spreading tree lest you become distracted, for the whole tree is within us. Its multiplicity is contained within our unity."
>
> Even, just as every seed, which is like the heart of the fruit, is a physical mirror confirming Divine unity, so it mentions and recites in the silent prayer of its heart the Divine Names the mighty tree recites in its audible prayer.
>
> Furthermore, just as the fruits and seeds are mirrors professing Divine unity, so they are the visible signs of Divine Determining and embodied tokens of Divine power. Through these words, Divine Determining and power intimate the following: "The many branches and twigs of this tree appeared from a single seed and demonstrate the unity of the tree's Artist in creating it and giving it form. Then, after growing and spreading its branches, it gathered together all its truths in a single fruit. It encapsulated its entire meaning in a single seed, thereby demonstrating the wisdom in the Glorious Creator's creation and planning."
>
> Similarly, the tree of the universe takes its existence from a source of unity and is sustained by it. And man, the fruit of the universe, demonstrates unity within this multiplicity of beings, while with the eye of faith his heart sees the mystery of unity within multiplicity.
>
> Moreover, the fruits and seeds are allusions of dominical wisdom. Wisdom says the following with them to those who are aware: "The comprehensive regard towards this tree and its

planning look with their comprehensiveness and universality to a single fruit. For the fruit is a miniature specimen of the tree. It is what is aimed at by the tree. Also, the comprehensive regard and planning look to every seed within the fruit, for the seed bears the meaning or index of the whole tree. That is to say, since the fruit is the aim of the tree's existence and the purpose of its creation, the One Who plans the tree regards each fruit with all His Names connected to the planning. Moreover, the mighty tree is sometimes pruned and trimmed for the sake of the tiny fruit; some parts of it are destroyed so that it may make new growth. It is grafted in order to produce even better, permanent fruit."

In the same way, man, who is the fruit of the tree of the universe, is the purpose of its creation and existence and the aim of the creation of beings. While his heart, which is the seed of the fruit, is a most brilliant and comprehensive mirror to the universe's Maker. It follows on from this wisdom, therefore, that tiny man will be the cause of the destruction and transformation of the universe. He will be the point of momentous revolutions like the Day of Resurrection. It will be for his judgement that the door of this world will be closed and that of the hereafter opened.

Since we have arrived at a discussion of resurrection, it is appropriate to explain one point concerning its reality which demonstrates the clarity and strength with which the Qur'an of Miraculous Exposition illuminates and proves resurrection.

The result yielded by this sequence of thought shows that if it is necessary for man's judgement and his gaining eternal happiness, the whole universe will be destroyed and that a power capable of destroying and transforming the universe shows itself and exists. But resurrection has many degrees. It is obligatory to believe in some of them; they must be acknowledged. Whereas others become apparent according to levels in spiritual and intellectual development, and for these knowledge pertaining to both are necessary.

In order to present cogent and strong proofs for the simplest and easiest level, the All-Wise Qur'an points out a power capable of opening up a truly vast realm of resurrection. The degree of resurrection in which it is necessary for all to believe is this:

After human beings die, their spirits depart for another realm. And their bodies rot except for a minute cell from the base of the spine which will act as a seed. It remains intact, and on the Day of Resurrection God Almighty will create the human body out of it and return its spirit to it. This degree is so simple, then, it may be seen every spring through millions of examples.

Sometimes in order to prove this degree, the verses of the Qur'an point out the unlimited activity of a power capable of raising to life all particles, and sometimes the traces of a power and wisdom capable of sending all creatures to extinction and then recalling them. Then they point to the activity and traces of a power and wisdom able to scatter the stars and shatter the heavens, and sometimes to the activity and manifestations of a power and wisdom capable of causing all animate creatures to die and then raising them to life again all at once at a single trumpet-blast.

Sometimes the verses demonstrate the manifestations of a power and wisdom that will raise to life the face of the earth and animate creatures all separately. And sometimes they demonstrate the traces of a power and wisdom that, lopping off its mountains, will cause the globe of the earth to disintegrate completely, and then restoring it will transform it into an even more excellent form.

That is to say, apart from the Day of Resurrection, in which it is obligatory for everyone to believe and to acknowledge, with that power and wisdom, God Almighty can create numerous other degrees and resurrections. And what is more, dominical wisdom requires that besides certainly bringing about mankind's resurrection, He shall bring about all those other degrees or create certain other important matters.[45]

Steps of Cultivating the Elements of Inward *Jihad*

In order to cultivate the elements of the spiritual path—impotence (*acz*), poverty (*fakr*), compassion (*şefkat*), and contemplation (*tefekkür*)—Nursi presents four steps (*hatves*). Basing each stage on different verses of the Qur'an, Nursi expands on each step as follows.

Step One

Inner *jihad*'s first stage, says Nursi, begins with the following qur'anic verse: "So do not claim yourselves to be pure."[46] Because of their nature and disposition (*cibilliyet* and *fitrat*), human beings love themselves (*nefislerini*). They prioritize the self, defend it always, and would sacrifice everything for it—as if it were worthy of worship. They may even think it is infallible. The

45. Nursi, *Words*, 640–43.
46. Qur'an 53:32.

faculties and skills given to them for the purpose of glorifying and offering thanks to God are used instead for selfish benefits of the soul. Such a person embodies the meaning of this qur'anic verse: "Who takes as his god his own desires."[47] At this stage, says Nursi, the necessary step to take is not self-purification, but self-absolution![48]

Step Two

Step two begins with reflection on the following qur'anic verse: "And be not like those who forgot God, so He made them forget themselves."[49] At this stage, Nursi explains, we forget and are not aware of our own selves. When we think about death, we think about the death of others, but not of our own. We see ephemeral things, but think that this ephemerality will not apply to us. When it comes to responsibility and serving, we forget that we have such obligations; however, in the case of rewards, benefits, and enjoyments, we always consider ourselves first. If we would purify our soul, Step Two requires that we forget self-interest and greed, thinking instead of our own mortality and the merit of serving others.[50]

Step Three

For step three, the motivating qur'anic verse, says Nursi, is "What comes to you of good is from God, but what comes to you of evil is from yourself."[51] The soul has the tendency to regard itself as the source of goodness. Such perception leads it to arrogance and egotism, Nursi asserts. The point of this third step is for the soul to see its impotence, faults, and poverty. One should know that all the beauties and good bestowed upon people are from God. Such perspective will lead the soul away from arrogance toward gratitude and thankfulness to God. Based on the message of the verse "Truly he succeeds who purifies it,"[52] purification at this stage takes the form of

---

47. Qur'an 25:43.
48. Nursi, *Words*, 492.
49. Qur'an 59:19.
50. Nursi, *Words*, 492.
51. Qur'an 4:79.
52. Qur'an 91:9.

knowing that perfection lies in imperfection, power in impotence, and wealth in poverty.[53]

Step Four

The fourth step is derived from this verse: "everything will perish save His countenance."[54] Nursi remarks that the soul thinks of itself as free, independent. It believes that its existence relies on nothing else. In a sense, the soul claims some divinity for itself. It revolts against its Creator. That the soul may be saved from such a grave error, Nursi offers this truth:

> According to the apparent meaning of things, which looks to each thing itself, everything is transitory, lacking, accidental, nonexistent. But according to the meaning that signifies something other than itself and in respect of each thing being a mirror to the All-Glorious Maker's Names and charged with various duties, each is a witness, it is witnessed, and it is existent.[55]

That is why, says Nursi—at this stage—if the soul relies on itself, but disregards the True Giver of Existence, then it will drown itself in unceasing separations and sufferings. But if the soul "gives up egotism and sees that he is a mirror of the manifestations of the True Giver of Existence," Nursi explains, then it "gains all beings and an infinite existence. For he who finds the Necessary Existent One, the manifestation of Whose Names all beings manifest, finds everything."[56]

Having described the steps of cultivating the elements of inward *jihad* and the stages necessary for reaching them, Nursi's interpretation of outward *jihad* and martyrdom are in order.

53. Nursi, *Words*, 493.
54. Qur'an 28:88.
55. Nursi, *Words*, 493.
56. Nursi, *Words*, 493.

Chapter 6

Enemies Redefined:
Nursi's Reinterpretation of Outward *Jihad*

SAID NURSI LIVED IN a time not unlike the early twenty-first century—a time when the term *jihad* was utilized intensely and continuously in Western journalism and polemic to describe brutalities attributed to Muslim extremists during confrontations with Western sovereignties in the Balkans, Greece, Armenia, Anatolia, Syria, and Lebanon.[1] As was explained earlier in this book, not only Westerners, but also some intellectuals within the Ottoman state who were highly critical of Islam, took part in this polemic.[2]

Nursi was cognizant of the crucial need for a new interpretation of *jihad*. Yes, he accepted the fact that, historically, the sword played a significant role in the spread of Islam.[3] However, he insisted that it should be understood in context—given the savagery of the era, such violence was part of societies.[4]

Nursi also asserts that human beings' desire for violence (*kuvve-i gadabiye*) has potential to be destructive: "people would potentially like to destroy everything they can, even the entire world when seen as an obstacle for their desire and greed."[5] The following of this desire for violence brings

---

1. Schleifer, "*Jihad*: Modernist Apologists, Modern Apologetics," 26–27.

2. As was mentioned earlier, Abdullah Cevdet, for instance, proposed embracing the Bahá'í faith as an alternative to the question of *jihad*.

3. Nursi, *İlk Dönem Eserleri*, 556.

4. Nursi, *İlk Dönem Eserleri*, 427.

5. Nursi, "Muhakemat," 2032.

forth tyrants like Pharaoh, Nimrod, and Shaddad.[6] One might add Hitler and Stalin to this category, too. Nursi believes that—properly understood— Islam changes this destructive habit into compassion. He gives an example from the Arabian society in the seventh century: "Yes, the Arabs whose hardness of heart caused them to bury their female children alive; however, through Islam their hearts were cleaned and waxed to the extent that they became so sensitive toward creatures that it prevented them from stepping on even ants."[7] Nursi believes that religion provides a mechanism with the capacity to control or change the course of violence.

That Nursi was well-aware of rapid globalization is indicated by his statement that the world has become like a small village[8]—and this in itself makes new interpretation of *jihad* a crucial matter. Nursi underscores that Muslims are now in a different period of time and civilization in which science and knowledge, rather than force and compulsion, should rule the world.[9] The attention he drew to rapid globalization seems to indicate that Nursi foresaw a time when homogenous societies would no longer exist, a time when interaction between the adherents of different religions and ethnicities would be easier than ever before. Therefore, a new theology of *jihad* that pursues harmony and coexistence—one capable of coping with the challenges of modernity—would be essential.

To understand Nursi's interpretation of *jihad*, it is helpful to take note of his exegesis of a Qur'an verse frequently cited in the context of critiques of calls for violence in Islam's scriptures. The verse in question reads: "God has purchased the persons and possessions of the believers in return for the Garden—they fight in God's way: they kill and are killed—this is a true promise given by Him in the Torah, the Gospel, and the Qur'an. Who could be more faithful to his promise than God? So be happy with the bargain you have made: that is the supreme triumph."[10] This verse is often interpreted in the sense that, literally, God has a covenant with the believers, a part of which is that they are to kill and be killed.[11] It is notable that, in commenting on this verse, to which his "Sixth Word" is devoted,[12] Nursi concentrates

6. Nursi, *Mesnevî-i Nuriye*, 261.

7. Nursi, "Muhakemat," 2032.

8. Nursi, *Mesnevî-i Nuriye*, 163.

9. Nursi, *İlk Dönem Eserleri*, 556.

10. Qur'an 9:111.

11. See Afsaruddin, *Striving in the Path of God*, 171–72.

12. Nursi, *Sözler*, 52–56.

on the first part of the verse—"God has purchased the persons and possessions of the believers in return for the Garden"—and offers a spiritual
meaning of this qur'anic instruction. He starts with an analogical story.

Nursi's commentary begins with a parable about a king who had en-
trusted a parcel of farmland and all equipment necessary for maintaining it
to each of two of his subjects. But now, war had come. In this state of emergency, nothing was stable; the likelihood that these subjects would lose the
property over which they were stewards was strong. So, the king sent his
main associate with a decree, offering these stewards the opportunity to
return to the king the responsibility for their farms until the emergency had
passed. The farms would then be returned to them. One subject found the
offer reasonable and accepted readily; the other, being egotistical, declined.
In the end, the person who accepted the offer was rewarded generously
by the king, while the one who had declined did lose everything and was
miserable.[13]

Nursi then explains the story. The king in the parable represents God.
The major associate is the Prophet Muhammad and the decree is the Qur'an.
The warlike situation represents this world. The farms and other tools sig-
nify the body of a human being and its faculties. The individual who loses
everything is an exemplar of the risk of following the vice of egotism; the
individual who was rewarded represents a person who chooses a God-
centered life—and such a life, Nursi asserts, has four distinct advantages:

1. It converts the finite into the infinite, in that it leads to eternal reward;

2. It provides assurance of the reality of heaven;

3. It enhances the value of all one's senses;[14]

4. It confers assurance that human beings, who are by nature weak and
   vulnerable, can overcome challenges through reliance on God.[15]

In this regard, Nursi's analogy for reading this verse is similar to al-Razi's
(d. 1210) commentary. In his *Tafsir al-Kabir*, Al-Razi comments that "a
subtlety of this verse [Q 9:111] is that in this profound transaction, God
is both the buyer and the seller, akin to the way an adult would transact

---

13. Nursi, *Sözler*, 53.

14. For example, eyesight used for worldly purposes only has its limits, but when it
is used to witness and contemplate the beautiful creation of God, its value is elevated.

15. Nursi, *Sözler*, 54–55.

the affairs of a helpless infant."[16] However, unlike many Qur'an exegetes, including al-Razi himself, Nursi leaves the second clause of the verse "they kill and are killed" aside, which has implications to physical, violent *jihad*. Instead, he derives a spiritual interpretation focusing entirely on spiritual *jihad*. For him, the core message of the verse in this age is mindfulness of and reliance on God. So seriously do the Muslims of the Nur community take Nursi's interpretation of this verse that they make it their practice to read what he has to say about it regularly during their gatherings.

Nursi's Interpretation of Martyrdom

In the new secular context of Turkey, Nursi often brings up the concept of martyrdom, which is usually associated with being killed in the fight for God. Referring to the status of the martyrs in Islam, the Qur'an states that people should "not say that those who are killed in God's cause are dead; they are alive, though you do not realize it."[17] Recall, however, that publishing the *Risale* was banned for decades; dissemination took place solely through writing and copying by hand. Not surprisingly, Nursi then considered the acts of writing and the copying of the *Risale* in the secular environment—and even simply studying it—to be as spiritually rewarding and of equal value to death for the cause of God.

In one of his letters to his less-committed students, Nursi points out that if a reader is dedicated to the *Risale* and follows the *sunna* (or "example") of Muhammad, this person can receive the reward of one hundred martyrs. To support his contention, he refers to two *hadiths* of Muhammad: that "anyone who follows my *sunna* when my community is corrupted shall receive the reward of a hundred martyrs";[18] and "the ink of scholars will be equal to the blood of martyrs on the day of judgment."[19] In Nursi's estimation, on the Day of Judgment, a single drop of ink flowing from the pen of a student writing out the *Risale* will carry the same benefit as one hundred drops of a martyr's blood. The martyrdom Nursi espouses results not from fighting against nonbelievers, but rather through engaging with his qur'anic commentary, the *Risale*, both individually and communally.

16. Nasr et al., *Study Qur'an*, 536.
17. Qur'an 2:154.
18. Nursi, *Lem'alar*, 278.
19. Nursi, *Lem'alar*, 278.

Said Nursi's Conceptualization of an Ethic of Nonviolence

Playing a key role in Nursi's design of an ethic of nonviolence is the notion of the scapegoat: one who bears all the blame for a bad situation, regardless of degree to which others have contributed. In his own formulation of *jihad*, which attempts to revive some aspects that had been dismissed or sidelined over the course of Islamic history, Nursi refuses to make scapegoats of "the West" or "non-Muslims;" contrary to much Islamic political theology, he avoids constructs such as the abode of Islam (*dar al-islam*) versus the abode of war (*dar al-harb*). Particular individuals and groups are not to be perceived as overarching threats, he says; rather, he draws attention to global enemies of concern to each and every group or individual. His pietist/quietist understanding of *jihad*, grounded in deeper underlying major qur'anic themes and the prophetic tradition, has two core elements: the sacred nature of human beings, and the principal that no soul shall bear the burden of another.

The Sacred Nature of Human Beings

Nursi begins with the fundamental belief that, since human beings are God's sacred creation, they are thus deserving of appreciation. This approach is based on the qur'anic verse: "We have honoured the children of Adam and carried them by land and sea; We have provided good sustenance for them and favoured them specially above many of those We have created."[20] In this regard, every individual is a manifestation of God's most beautiful names (*al-asma al-husna*), the divine attributes so often mentioned in the Qur'an; every person is a reflection of God's qualities and a unique combination of these divine characteristics. Thus, every person is, in a sense, sacred. Nursi says that every person desires to show and enjoy his/her skills; similarly, God wants to see the beauty of his attributes in his creatures.[21]

The creatures of God, says Nursi, can be perceived in two ways. From the "self-referential" (*manay-ı ismî*) perspective, one regards the creatures as they indicate their own existence. Their divine origin is not recognized. From the "other-indicative" (*manay-ı harfî*) vantage point, various signs can be perceived that point to their Creator, and which all creatures carry. Nursi strongly encourages people to look at the creatures from this second

20. Qur'an 17:70.
21. Nursi, *Şu'alar*, 118.

perspective.[22] If one wants to show one's amazement, Nursi discourages exclamations about creatures such as "How beautiful they are," preferring that people say "how beautifully they have been made! How exquisitely they point to their Maker's beauty!"[23] For him, the Maker should always be taken into consideration.[24] The simple but fundamental fact that human beings are created by God and are embodiments of his beautiful names excludes violence as appropriate behavior toward human beings. Such conduct would be a denial and rejection of God's beautiful art.

The Qur'anic Principle: "No soul shall bear the burden of another soul"

Also crucial to Nursi's advocacy of nonviolence is his understanding of the divine assertion "No soul shall bear the burden of another soul," which appears in four chapters of the Qur'an,[25] and to which he refers more than a dozen times in his writings. As Nursi explains this verse, no one's shortcomings are to be the basis of judgment against them. The faults or mistakes of an individual cannot be assumed by someone else. Consequently, no one is to be made a scapegoat for someone else's crime. To illustrate, Nursi—employing a principle of "absolute justice" (adalet-i mahza) instead of "relative justice" (adalet-i izafiye)[26]—offers a parable of a ship with ten passengers, nine of whom have committed serious crimes and one of whom is innocent. The presence of nine guilty parties would not justify the burning or sinking of this ship; the goal does not justify the means if an innocent person will be killed in the process.[27] In a society in which perfect justice flourishes, he insists, an innocent person cannot be chosen as a scapegoat to be sacrificed for the whole community.[28] In this way, Nursi closes the doors particularly for self-declared militant jihadists who commit violent acts against innocent civilians. Based on this qur'anic principle, neighbors, relatives, and fellow human beings in general cannot be held accountable

22. Nursi, *Words*, 145.
23. Nursi, *Words*, 145.
24. Nursi, *Words*, 145.
25. Qur'an 17:15; Qur'an 6:164; Qur'an 35:18; Qur'an 39:7.
26. Nursi, "Sunuhat," 320.
27. Nursi, *Emirdağ Lahikasi II*, 1882.
28. Nursi, *Emirdağ Lahikasi II*, 1844.

for another person's evil acts. The individuality of a crime needs to be considered.[29] Collective punishment can never be an option.

Nursi's answer to the question of why the Muslim world was facing so many calamities, including the devastation of World War I, was to resist assigning blame externally. Instead, he would remind his followers that God asks the believers to spend one hour a day in ritual prayer; instead, they had been overcome by laziness and did not fulfill that request. So, through military drills and hardships, God made them pray. Furthermore, God asked the pious to fast one month a year, but instead the command was ignored; God asked for them to give the obligatory alms-tax (*zakat*), but people disobeyed. So, God took all the charities that the believers were supposed to give.[30] The causes of all calamities, according to Nursi, rested with Muslims themselves.

Nursi thus refrains from designating particular individuals and categories of people (such as non-Muslims) as enemies. The enemies to which he points instead are ignorance, conflict, poverty, and unbelief. Nursi attempts to unify various elements of society in order to strive collectively against those threats.

Jihad against Ignorance

For Nursi, ignorance, prevalent not only in non-Muslim but also Muslim communities, is to be a primary target—to be combated by promotion of learning.[31] On the basis of the scriptural mandate, "Call to the way of your Lord with wisdom and beautiful discourse and debate with them in the best way,"[32] he developed a curriculum founded on principles of quietism and *ihsan* (doing things beautifully for God alone). Central to it were teachings supporting his preference for "spiritual" (as opposed to "violent") *jihad*—for example, by pointing to such *hadiths* as "The ink of scholars will have the same value as the blood of martyrdoms on the Day of Judgment"[33] (which we have just considered); or, "during the time of the innovations and aberrations those who follow my *sunna* (the way of the Prophet of Islam)

29. Nursi, *Emirdağ Lahikasi II*, 1844.

30. Nursi, *Ilk Dönem Eserleri*, 345.

31. Nursi, *Ilk Dönem Eserleri*, 396.

32. Qur'an 16:24.

33. al-Suyuti, *al-Jami' al-Saghir*, no. 1006; Al-'Ajluni, *Kashf al-Khafa*, 261; cited in Nursi, *Emirdağ Lahikası I*, 246.

and the truth of the Qur'an, their deeds are the equivalent of one hundred martyrs."[34] Because he regarded intellectual persuasion by word and tongue as the most influential way of teaching, Nursi asserted that, in a civilized world, "the way to defeat civilized people is the way of persuasion, and not the way of force, which is applied to those people who don't understand words."[35]

Jihad against Unbelief and Conflict

Through his *Risale*, Nursi advocated "peaceful *jihad*" or "*jihad* of the word" (*manevî jihad*) in the struggle against aggressive atheism and irreligion," explains his biographer Şükran Vahide. By working solely for the spread and strengthening of belief, it was to work also for the preservation of internal order and justice and peace in society in the face of the moral and spiritual destruction by communism and the forces of irreligion which aimed to destabilize society and create anarchy, and to form "a barrier" against them.[36]

By condemning the *jihad* of the sword or military *jihad*, Nursi positioned a peaceful struggle in the center of his writings. He constantly encouraged his students to promote peace and harmony in society in the manner of "positive action" (*müsbet hareket*), the details of which we considered in chapter 4 above.

In one of his letters from Emirdağ, we read, "Our duty is 'positive action,' not 'negative action.' It is solely to serve belief [in the truths of religion] in accordance with divine pleasure, and not to interfere in God's concerns." The result of such positive service to belief, he explains, is "the preservation of public order and security."[37] In another letter to his students, Nursi writes that "the most important duty of the *Risale-i Nur* students at this time is taking *taqwa* [God-consciousness] as the basis of their actions against moral destruction."[38] Nursi leaves no room for conflict, which might lead to disorder, chaos, and anarchy—thus contradicting God's desire for order and unity.

---

34. al-Munzere, *at-Targhib wa Tarhib*, 1:41; Tabarane, *al-Macmau'l-Kaber*, 1394, cited in Nursi, *Emirdağ Lahikası I*, 246.

35. Nursi, *Bediüzzaman'ın Tarihçe-i Hayatı*, 77.

36. Vahide, *Author of the Risale-i Nur*, 352.

37. Nursi, *Emirdağ Lahikası II*, 630.

38. Nursi, *Kastamonu Lahikası*, 186.

Jihad against Hatred

Nursi acknowledged that human beings have the potential to be destructive and hateful, but asserted that what is most worthy of being hated is hatred itself. In his well-known Damascus Sermon, Nursi says:

> What I am certain of from my experience of social life and have learnt from my life-time of study is the following: the thing most worthy of love is love, and that most deserving of enmity is enmity. That is, love and loving, which renders man's social life secure and lead to happiness are most worthy of love and being loved. Enmity and hostility are ugly and damaging, have overturned man's social life, and more than anything deserve loathing and enmity and to be shunned.[39]

Elsewhere, he states that "we are competitors of love; we have no time for enmity."[40]

If hatred is the infection, then—for Nursi—compassion is the antidote. If one encounters an enemy (or even a person who simply has shortcomings), compassion, rather than hatred, is the best means of approach. As Nursi states in his *Rays* collection, students of the *Risale-i Nur* "feel not anger at their enemies, but pity and compassion. They try to reform them in the hope they shall be saved."[41] As he sees it, compassion is a highly significant faculty of the human heart. If human hearts are devoid of respect and compassion, "reason and intellect would make human beings such horrible and cruel monsters to the extent that they would not be able to be ruled by politics anymore."[42]

Several incidents in Nursi's life demonstrate his compassionate attitude. According to his student Süleyman Hünkar, he and Nursi were among some 350 to 400 inmates in Denizli Prison in southwestern Turkey—most of whom were guilty of murder and among whom fights and quarrels were commonplace and often ended in violence. In fact, 18 prisoners were killed between 1939 (the year in which Hünkar himself was incarcerated) and 1943 (the year in which Nursi and 126 of his students joined him there).[43] According to Hünkar, Nursi's impact on his fellow prisoners was almost

39. Nursi, *Damascus Sermon*, 49.
40. Nursi, *İlk Dönem Eserleri*, 426.
41. Nursi, *Rays*, 290.
42. Nursi, "Şualar," 888.
43. Şahiner, "Süleyman Hünkar Maddesi," 268–73.

remarkably transformative. Even convicted murderers were now hesitant to kill little insects out of their newfound understanding of compassion and love for God's creatures.[44]

A final example stems from the period Nursi called that of the "Old Said"—the period before his mental and spiritual transformation in 1921. During the Russian occupation in the eastern province of the Ottoman Empire, Armenians were attacking villages like Isparit, a place close to Nursi's hometown of Nurs. The troops under Nursi's command were able to suppress the Armenian forces. Nursi gathered the Armenian women and children in the area and handed them over to the Armenian forces.[45] In a time of major upheavals and tensions between Muslims and Armenians in the region, Nursi declined an opportunity to kill innocent Armenian civilians. According to Abdurrahman, another biographer of Nursi, the Armenians were so impressed by his compassionate behavior that they refrained from killing innocent civilians on the enemy side.[46]

Thus, we see how Nursi redefined threats toward and enemies of the Muslim community—indeed toward civilization at large—as ignorance, conflict, hatred, and unbelief. Using force and sword in order to elevate the religion of Islam was no longer valid, in his estimation; instead, preference is given to persuasion and communication by means of intellectual endeavors. Compassion and love are at the core elements of his new method. How, then, does this method bear upon Nursi's attitude toward non-Muslims, particularly Christians? That is a question worth considering.

Nursi on Religious Diversity: His View of Christians

To recall, Nursi refrained from targeting particular groups. Thus, unsurprisingly, he promoted unity between the adherents of the two major traditions of Islam and Christianity. Nursi states that there is a distinction between one's personality and one's attributes; "a person is loved not for his personhood, but for his character."[47] He then elaborates on some negative characteristics of Muslims that are not Islamic and do not deserve to be loved. He says that, just as "it is not necessarily so that every attribute of

44. Şahiner, "Süleyman Hünkar Maddesi," 268–73.
45. Nursi, *Bedîüzzaman'ın Tarihçe-i Hayatı*, 36.
46. Nursi, *Bedîüzzaman'ın Tarihçe-i Hayatı*, 36.
47. Nursi, *İlk Dönem Eserleri*, 483.

every Muslim is Muslim, it is not necessarily so that every attribute of every non-Muslim is non-Muslim."[48]

As noted, after the redeclaration of the Turkish constitution (*II Meşrutiyet*) in 1908, Nursi travelled to different parts of the eastern province of the empire in order to "enlighten" people about freedom. As was explained in chapter 1, many tribes were concerned about new developments, such as the right of an Armenian to become a governor. Nursi's response was progressive: he believed that a person's religious affiliation should not be a detriment to their opportunities for leadership or involvement in government. At that time, he explains, "The Armenians have certain jobs such as horologer or machinist in this country; likewise, they can become governors. The governors are the paid servants of the people if there is a precise constitution."[49] Constitutional principles need to be followed in any case. Again, the issue is not one's religion, but one's skills.

Immediately after World War II, Nursi asserted that "believers should now unite, not only with their Muslim fellow-believers, but with truly religious and pious Christians, disregarding questions of [theological] dispute and not arguing over them, for absolute disbelief is on the attack."[50] Thus, Nursi encouraged Muslims and Christians to work together for social justice and against threats to faith and spirituality. Nursi put his words into action. In 1950, he sent a collection of his writings to Pope Pius XII; on February 22, 1951, he received a personal letter of thanks.[51] It is important to note that the successor of Pope Pius, Pope John XXIII (d. 1963), who became pope in 1958, served as the Apostolic Delegate of the Holy See at Istanbul from 1934 to 1944.[52] Living in a Muslim majority country, Pope John XXIII was fluent in Turkish and, because of his love for Turkish culture and people, was also known as "the Turkish Pope." Considering that Nursi was a public figure and receiving a lot of attention from media and government because of his struggle for freedom of religion during Pope John XXIII's residence in Turkey, it is highly likely that the pope knew about Nursi and his works.

On January 25, 1959, Pope John XXIII called for the Second Vatican Council. As a result of the council, the Catholic Church revised its

48. Nursi, *İlk Dönem Eserleri*, 483.

49. Nursi, *Bediüzzaman'ın Tarihçe-i Hayatı*, 478.

50. Nursi, *Emirdağ Lahikası I*, 265.

51. Nursi, *Emirdağ Lahikası II*, 433.

52. For more about Pope John XXIII's time in Turkey, see Faggioli, *John XXIII*, 68–78.

relationship with non-Christian religions, particularly Jews and Muslims, through the declaration known as *Nostra Aetate*. Concerning Muslims, the council declared:

> The Church regards with esteem also the Moslems. They adore the one God, living and subsisting in Himself; merciful and all-powerful, the Creator of heaven and earth, who has spoken to men; they take pains to submit wholeheartedly to even His inscrutable decrees, just as Abraham, with whom the faith of Islam takes pleasure in linking itself, submitted to God. Though they do not acknowledge Jesus as God, they revere Him as a prophet. They also honor Mary, His virgin Mother; at times they even call on her with devotion. In addition, they await the Day of Judgment when God will render their deserts to all those who have been raised up from the dead. Finally, they value the moral life and worship God especially through prayer, almsgiving and fasting.

In addition, more than a decade after Nursi's call for cooperation between Muslims and Christians in dealing with the challenges to faith in the modern age, the Council also called for a mutual effort between the adherents of the two faiths: "Since in the course of centuries not a few quarrels and hostilities have arisen between Christians and Moslems, this sacred synod urges all to forget the past and to work sincerely for mutual understanding and to preserve as well as to promote together for the benefit of all mankind social justice and moral welfare, as well as peace and freedom."[53]

According to Thomas Michel, though there is no official document to prove the correlation, Nursi's efforts may well have had direct impact on the Second Vatican Council, in that it was only a bit more than a decade after Nursi's correspondence with the Pope that, during Vatican II, "the Catholic Church proclaimed its respect and esteem for Muslims and asserted that Islam was a genuine path of salvation."[54] Nursi also visited the Ecumenical Patriarch Athenagoras in Istanbul in 1953, in order to seek cooperation between Muslims and Christians against threats to faith and spirituality.[55]

Clearly, Nursi considered Christians to be allies rather than threats or targets. He believed that humanity was facing a different age; therefore,

53. For the declaration, see "Nostra Aetate," http://www.vatican.va/archive/hist_councils/ii_vatican_council/documents/vat-ii_decl_19651028_nostra-aetate_en.html.

54. Michel, *Said Nursi's Views*, 36.

55. Şahiner, *Bilinmeyen Taraflarıyla*, 372–73. See also Vahide, *Islam in Modern Turkey*, 317.

Muslim perception of non-Muslims should be changed. In interpreting the verse, "O you who believe! Do not take the Jews and the Christians for your friends and protectors,"[56] Nursi observes that during Muhammad's time people's minds were very much occupied with religion; therefore, "love and hatred were concentrated on that point and they loved or hated accordingly."[57] However, in the twentieth century, people's minds were occupied more with worldly affairs. "Our friendship with Christians is because of our admiration for their civilization and progress," he asserts. "Therefore, such friendship is certainly not included in the qur'anic prohibition."[58] He calls for a more nuanced understanding of religious believers: "Just as not all of the characteristics of an individual Muslim necessarily reflect the teaching of Islam, so also, not all of the qualities of individual Jews and Christians reflect unbelief."[59] If Muslims find in a Jew or Christian qualities that are in agreement with Islamic teaching, they should consider these qualities praiseworthy. It is those good qualities that form the basis for a friendship with Jews and Christians. Nursi then asks the question "Can a Muslim love a Christian or Jew?" Answering his own question, he avers, "Of course!"[60] As Michel rightly explains, "Nursi's argument is that the very fact that the Qur'an permits a Muslim man to marry a Jewish or Christian woman presumes that he can and should love her."[61] It is also noteworthy to mention again Nursi's reflections on the innocent Christians who lost their lives during the years of World War II. Nursi considered all who died in that conflict to be "martyrs of a sort, whatever religion they belonged to," adding that "their reward would be great and likely save them from Hell," and concluding that "it may be said with certainty that the calamity which the oppressed among Christians suffer, those connected to Jesus . . . is a sort of martyrdom for them."[62]

It is also important to note that Nursi's view in this context drew criticism from some Muslims in Turkey arguing that it is not grounded in orthodox Islam. In fact, this became an important question within the Muslim community in Turkey after Nursi's death. For example, Necip Fazıl

56. Qur'an 5:51.
57. Nursi, *İlk Dönem Eserleri*, 483–84.
58. Nursi, *İlk Dönem Eserleri*, 483–84.
59. Nursi, *İlk Dönem Eserleri*, 483–84.
60. Nursi, *İlk Dönem Eserleri*, 483–84.
61. Michel, *Said Nursi's Views*, 38.
62. Nursi, *Kastamonu Lahikası*, 141.

Kısakürek (d. 1983), one of the most public figures among Muslims in Turkey in the seventies, wrote an article denouncing Nursi's view of salvation concerning non-Muslims.[63] After Kısakürek's article, the leading students of Nursi met him. The discussion clarified that Nursi's view of non-Muslims' salvation were very much in line with al-Ghazali's (d. 1111), one of the most respected theologians in the Muslim tradition.[64] Kısakürek then wrote another article the next day and revised his criticism.[65]

Conclusion

This chapter attempted to demonstrate Nursi's ethic of nonviolence and his views of outward *jihad*, martyrdom, and people of other religions. Nursi believed that human nature has a tendency toward violence. He also accepted the fact that, historically, Muslims had indeed used "the sword" as a means to accomplish their goals. In this sense, Nursi is not apologetic. He was also well aware that physical struggle is not something peculiar to Islamic societies alone. Therefore, context must always be taken into consideration.

Nursi believed that, by the twentieth century, humanity had reached a new plateau—an era of civilization and knowledge. Violent *jihad* was no longer appropriate as a means for spreading Islam, nor is it any longer appropriate to make scapegoats of Christians and Jews (or Westerners *per se*) for the deficiencies of the situation in which Muslim find themselves. In the era of civilization, "persuasion" is the most efficient way to deal with non-Muslims—who are, he asserts, potential allies of Muslims in the promotion of peace and justice in the world and the struggle against unbelief. Persons are to be evaluated in terms of their attributes rather than their religious affiliation. Thus, Nursi develops a *jihad* against the threats of ignorance, conflict, unbelief, and hatred. He strives against them with knowledge, positive action, belief, and compassion.

---

63. For the Nur community's reaction to Kısakürek's article, see Kırkıncı, *Hayatım-Hatıralarım*, 299.

64. For more details about Ghazali's view on the fate of non-Muslims, see al-Ghazali, *On the Boundaries of Theological Tolerance*.

65. Kırkıncı, *Hayatım-Hatıralarım*, 299.

Chapter 7

Guidelines for the Community of Believers

Service to Faith in Pursuit of Divine Pleasure

IN VARIOUS PLACES IN the *Risale*, Nursi states that the motivation behind service in religious matters is the quest for divine pleasure. Sincerity (*ikhlās*)—or doing service for the sake of God—is the essence of the work of the community of believers. They should have no other goal or expectation in the service of faith, nor should they reap any worldly gain. In his treatise on sincerity, Nursi presents four basic principles for attaining this virtue:[1]

1. In your deeds and actions, you seek nothing but divine pleasure (*ikhlās*).

2. Do not criticize those who are with you in the service and do not make them jealous by showing off your virtues.

3. Believe that strength lies in sincerity and truth.

4. Be proud of the skills and merits of the people who are with you in service as if they are your own.

Nursi also presents the obstacles in cultivating sincerity while on the path of service to faith:

1. Nursi, *Lem'alar*, 267–77.

103

a. Seeking material advantage in doing service.

b. Flattering and praising the ego and soul.

c. Seeking attention of people for fame and worldly positions.

d. Being occupied with fear and greed.[2]

Perhaps one of the most important of Nursi's practices in meeting the principles of sincerity was his refusal to accept gifts from people, including his own followers.[3] As a prominent figure, whether to accept tangible expressions of appreciation from even the closest of his thousands of students was a recurring question. Nursi therefore wrote a section in the *Risale* explaining why he declined gifts. In short, he believed that receiving gifts because of his service to religion would harm his sincerity in serving. He pointed out that he even declined the gifts from his brother Abdulmecid and nephew Abdurrahman.

In offering a detailed rationale, Nursi begins with a reminder that among those who oppose religion are some who accuse religious scholars of "exploiting knowledge and religion to make a living for themselves."[4] Nursi sought to disprove their accusation in practice. Second, he notes that, for Muslims, service to religion means following the example of the prophets, and their practice accords with the Qur'an's assertion that "My reward is only due from God."[5] Furthermore, the Qur'an teaches the believers to "follow those who ask no reward" in exchange for their teachings.[6]

Third, he insists that one should give and receive for the sake of God: "Whereas mostly either the one giving is heedless and gives in his own name and implicitly puts the recipient under an obligation, or the recipient is heedless; he gives the thanks and praise due to the True Provider to apparent causes and is in error."[7] Fourth, reliance on God, contentment, and frugality are, in Nursi's mind, great treasures for which there is no adequate exchange. Receipt of gifts and wealth from people closes doors to these treasures. He writes, "I have been following this principle from my childhood and would continue to follow for the remaining of my life as well."[8]

2. Nursi, *Lem'alar*, 267–77.

3. Nursi, *Letters*, 30–32.

4. Nursi, *Letters*, 31.

5. Qur'an 10:72.

6. See Qur'an 36:21.

7. Nursi, *Letters*, 29.

8. Nursi, *Letters*, 29.

Fifth, a series of experiences and signs during his service to faith caused Nursi to conclude that he was not permitted to accept gifts from the rich and officials.[9] Furthermore, he noted, gifts never come without expectations attached: whenever people give, they hope that they might receive both spiritual and worldly benefits by having given gifts. Sixth, Nursi refers to an assertion by Ibn Hajar al-Haytami (d. 1566) that "if you are not righteous it is forbidden to accept something intended for the righteous."[10] If, God forbid, "I [Nursi] consider myself to be righteous, it is a sign of pride and points to the absence of righteousness. If I do not consider myself to be righteous, it is not permissible to accept those goods."[11]

By eschewing service to faith as a means for personal gain, Nursi maximized frugality. People would ask him, "How do you live? What do you live on since you do not work? We don't want people in our country who sit around idly and live off the labour of others."[12] Nursi would answer that he had reduced his expenses to the minimum. For example, Nursi writes, "I bought this coat I'm wearing seven years ago second-hand. In five years, I have spent only four and a half liras on clothes, underwear, slippers, and stockings. Frugality and divine mercy and the resulting plenty have sufficed me."[13] Having dedicated his entire life to the service of faith, Nursi owned nearly nothing. In fact, when Nursi died in 1960 in the city of Urfa, the value of his personal effects—"his watch, gown, prayer-mat, tea-pot and glasses, and a few odds and ends," all of which could be carried in a single basket—was noted by the estate lawyer as 551 liras and 50 kuruş.[14]

Avoidance of Politics

The second core guideline for the community of believers is avoidance of politics. In fact, to this day, "I seek refuge in God from politics and satan" has become a mantra among the students of Nursi. As noted in previous chapters, Nursi initially had hope in politics as a means to save the Ottoman Empire from collapse and to serve the larger Muslim community. To his great disappointment, the empire was dismantled and the situation of

9. Nursi, *Letters*, 29.
10. Nursi, *Letters*, 30.
11. Nursi, *Letters*, 30.
12. Nursi, *Letters*, 88.
13. Nursi, *Letters*, 89.
14. Vahide, *Author of the Risale-i Nur*, 374.

the global Muslim community grew even worse.[15] During the Second Said period, he then strongly urged the students of the *Risale* to avoid politics. Nursi repeatedly stated that the service to religion should never be used as a means for politics. Rather, service to faith and religion is above politics—which is, he was certain—a major obstacle in the way of people's access to spirituality.[16] Politics cannot be a priority of the community of faith, he insisted; nor should the Qur'an be used for political means. His own priority was to strengthen believers' faith in the new secular and modern context.

At various points in the *Risale*, Nursi offers specific reasons for avoidance of politics. In the first place, it divides rather than unites—especially when it comes to religious matters. To make his point, Nursi shares a story from his own circle:

> I once saw, as a result of biased partisanship, a pious scholar of religion going so far in his condemnation of another scholar with whose political opinions he disagreed as to imply that he was an unbeliever. He also praised with respect a dissembler who shared his own opinions. I was appalled at these evil results of political involvement. I said: "I take refuge in God from Satan and politics," and from that time on withdrew from politics.[17]

Referring to this anecdote in another place in the *Risale*, Nursi remarks further that he warned the pious scholar that "if Satan would support your political ideas, you would interpret it as God's mercy; however even if the one who disagrees with you would be an angel, you would curse him."[18] With this story, Nursi shows how politics can be a great source of division, even among pious Muslim scholars. In politics, what too often matters is not being on the side of truth, but rather being with anyone who is in agreement with one's own political opinion.

In the second place, involvement in politics may lead to injustice—and this would be contrary to core principles of the *Risale* such as compassion, justice, truth, and consciousness. Nursi points out that, for example, when you punish someone through politics because of their disbelief, you are also keeping away at least seven or eight people—the offender's children, spouse, the sick, the elderly, and innocent bystanders—from religion!

15. Nursi, *Sikke-i Tasdik-i Gaybî*, 265.
16. Nursi, *Bediüzzaman'ın Tarihçe-i Hayatı*, 691. See also Nursi, *Mektubat*, 81.
17. Nursi, *Bediüzzaman'ın Tarihçe-i Hayatı*, 93.
18. Nursi, *Bediüzzaman'ın Tarihçe-i Hayatı*, 123.

Harm to one person causes collateral harm to others.[19] Even if sinning or causing others to sin were merely "a one or two in ten possibility," the risk of collateral harm would be too great, says Nursi[20]—which, he once said, is why he gave up reading newspapers, involvement in politics, and even worldly conversation about politics.[21]

Finally, Nursi repeatedly emphasizes the prophetic principle that "Power is in right; right is not in power."[22] It is difficult to follow this principle in politics, he notes, because politics too often follows the principle "Might is right" or "All power to the strongest."[23]

Non-Hierarchy

Another guideline from Nursi to the community of believers is the notion of avoiding a hierarchy among the members of the community. In fact, he starts with himself. Often, when his followers would come to visit him, he would decline to meet them, referring them to the *Risale* itself instead. Thus, he formed a text-based faith community. To this day, members of the Nur community come together for the sake of God to read and discuss the *Risale* for its own sake—not for any material gain.

To reinforce his non-hierarchical stance, Nursi went so far as to instruct his followers that no one should know the place of his grave, so that people would not come to visit him as a saint. At a time when many people are hypocritically seeking fame and popularity, maximum sincerity demands that believers should renounce arrogance and egotism completely. "People who respect me," Nursi continues, can pray for me from a distance. "They should not visit my graveyard. Dismantling my egotism through maximum sincerity requires me to say this."[24]

The sign of the non-hierarchical nature of the Nur community is that it is not centralized. People organize locally, come together informally, and read the *Risale* in a place of study known as a *dersane*, or even in their private homes. A family of two can even gather around the reading. Material and formal structures or institutions are not a requirement for establishing

19. Nursi, *Bediüzzaman'ın Tarihçe-i Hayatı*, 691.
20. Nursi, *Letters*, 84.
21. Nursi, *Letters*, 84.
22. Nursi, *Words*, 563.
23. Nursi, *Words*, 563.
24. Nursi, *Emirdağ Lahikası II*, 588.

a spiritual gathering. Formal membership is nonexistent; the circle remains open to people from all walks of life. There are no prerequisites to fulfill to enter the gathering.

Finally, eschewal of hierarchy means that the path of the *Risale* has no position of *shaykh* as do the Islamic orders (*tariqa*). In this regard, Nursi believed that institutional Sufism cannot address the problems of the Muslim world. What was at stake in this age is faith (*iman*). Nursi thus stated that "one can enter heaven without Sufism, however one can not enter heaven without faith (*iman*)." Sufism is secondary compared to faith. This is what people need at this time. Yet, there are many aspects of the *Risale* that are compatible with Sufism. Nursi has benefitted from the essence of Sufism, but has left behind its hierarchical structure.

Were the Nur community to recognize the position of *shaykh*, by definition only one such position would be available. Many people would long for this position, Nursi observed. Thus, even though the holder of this position is intended to be a spiritual guide for others, selfishness and envy in relation to this office could not be avoided. The resulting conflicts and divisions within the community of believers would without a doubt be harmful for their spirituality. On the other hand, the Nur way, says Nursi, is brotherhood/sisterhood. Siblings help and support each other. Among siblings, no one is in the position of father or spiritual guide; there is no hierarchy, no spiritual leader.[25]

Community vs. Individualism

One of the focuses of Nursi and his *Risale* was forming a bonding community in a secular environment through the *dershane* gatherings. From the early years of the Nur community's inception, the readers of the *Risale* have come together in apartment houses known as *dershanes*. They read and discuss the themes of the *Risale*. These *dershanes* not only offered a counter narrative that made a case for faith, but also played a significant role in forming a bonding community of believers.

It is important to note that the "communal expression of faith" has been losing ground in many contexts. We see that this is more the case in societies where modernity and secularism are dominant. Instead, "the individualistic expression of faith" has become more important. One of the most important aspects of religion is that it provides a sense of belonging.

25. Nursi, *Letters*, 220.

With gradual secularization, the "believing without belonging" approach increasingly draws followers.[26] A growing number of people in the United States, for instance, do not identify with any religious group.[27]

In such a context, believers need creative ways to form a bonding community. Meeting in small groups for solidarity and forming a community becomes crucial to survive spiritually in a secular context. In order to illustrate some examples from the United States, one can name Brian McLaren as one of the most prominent pastors in America. In 2005, McLaren was listed among the twenty-five most influential evangelical Christians in America. He founded the Cedar Ridge Community Church, and within a short time he was able to appeal to hundreds of "uncharged" people. It is remarkable that the community started in a little apartment. While working as an English professor at the university, McLaren and his wife would invite people to their apartment for spiritual gatherings. All they did was pray together, read the Bible, and share a meal.[28] In fact, there are so many cases like McLaren's, especially within the evangelical community. The churches would start with a few people reading the Bible at home.

Similar challenges of modernity and secularism concerning faith and spirituality in modern Turkey can be cited as well, although to a different degree. The challenge becomes more apparent, particularly in highly urbanized metropolitan areas. The relational dynamics have changed in these places.

In this context, the spiritual gatherings at *dershanes* provide a way for building a safe and trustful community. The fact that most of the attendees at *dershanes* are not born in megacities like Istanbul is a testimony to these observations. Communal relations acquired through *dershanes* become a substitute for close relationships. As previously noted, religious institutions where believers would come together for spiritual purposes were dismantled and religion banned from the public sphere. Hence *dershanes* became the platform for Muslim believers to come together around the readings of the *Risale*, form strong bonds, and keep hope under such severe circumstances. Simply coming together was already perceived as a rebellion by the regime and could result in persecution. As one of the students

---

26. Steinfels, "Modernity and Belief," https://www.commonwealmagazine.org/modernity-belief.

27. Lipka, "Why America's 'Nones' Left Religion," http://www.pewresearch.org/fact-tank/2016/08/24/why-americas-nones-left-religion-behind/.

28. Blackwell, "Return or Rereading," 17.

of Nursi put it, going to *dershanes* in the evenings meant that there was a 50 percent chance of returning home after the session. The other option was to end up in jail.[29]

Nursi's statement, "this time is the time of community engagement," has become a mantra among his followers. He believes that in this age it is almost impossible for believers to remain spiritual and preserve their faith individually. The reason for that is the collective attack on faith and spirituality. He maintains that the castles surrounding faith are being damaged. Believers have a fragile faith.[30] To his mind, collective gatherings are necessary for the strengthening of individual faith. Nursi believes that even if a person is very pious, it is impossible for that person to maintain a spiritual life with a firm belief since the attack on religion is collective.[31] To a collective attack, a profound response should be a collective one (*şahs-ı mânevî*). Only through a collective personality, a person can overcome the challenges to faith and spirituality. The concern of a believer should not be individualism and self, but rather collective personality manifested in the community. This ultimately leads to enhance the individual self by gaining a larger identity through a collective one. To further make his point, Nursi uses an example of a pool of water and an ice cube thrown into it to be melted. In this case, the pool represents a collective personality, while the piece of ice represents individualism and ego. Individuals should throw and melt their individual personality and ego in the pool. As a result, one will gain a larger understanding of one's self than before. To reiterate, this does not mean complete annihilation of the self though.[32]

Nursi believes that a collective personality formed around the readings of the *Risale* can overcome the challenges to faith and spirituality. While it is possible that reading the *Risale* individually can still form this personality, it is mainly manifested in the collective readings in *dershanes*.

On a weekly basis, the readers of the *Risale* gather in *dershanes* to read and study the texts. Because these reflective exercises are usually undertaken in small groups, over the course of time the gatherings form a community with strong bonds and close relations. It has also been shown that these circles have strengthened civic society in Turkey as people get together frequently and build relationships of mutual trust and responsibility.

29. My interview with Mehmet Fırıncı on March 25, 2017.
30. Nursi, *Mektubat*, 661.
31. Nursi, *Kastamonu Lahikası*, 180.
32. Nursi, *Kastamonu Lahikası*, 180.

Taking care of one another and exchanging common concerns in the process of deep sharing helps to alleviate a multitude of mental health issues.[33]

Notably, Nursi argues that if these spiritual sessions are done sincerely and for the sake of God, collective spiritual works may bear fruits, like the way collective worldly works give results. Nursi clarifies his point with the example of making a lamp. Imagine, Nursi says, five people come together to craft an old-style lamp. One comes with paraffin, another brings a wick, still another person provides the lamp, the fourth person offers the mantle, and then the fifth person comes with the matches. They put together the lamp and light it. Because it is a collective accomplishment, each of them becomes the owner of the lamp. If each of these persons holds a proper mirror to the lamp, the light of it would be fully reflected in their mirrors. Nursi's other analogy is manufacturing needles. In this example, there are ten manufacturers and they work individually. Each of them is able to manufacture three needles. They then decide to unite their work and work collectively: "One brought the iron, one lit the furnace, one pierced the needles, one placed them in the furnace, and another sharpened the points, and so on; each was occupied with only part of the process of needle-making."[34] With their collective work, they used their time more efficiently and were able to produce three hundred needles.[35]

Nursi then concludes that the collectively done spiritual work is no different than the worldly one. This way, the work is multiplied with collective work, in the same way that spiritual works bear multiple fruits. Collective spiritual work is more efficient and productive than individually performed spiritual works. However, Nursi warns that, as in the worldly works, if there is rivalry and insincerity involved in the collective work, it will jeopardize the result; the same thing can be said for the collective spiritual work. Bonds among the members of the community thus should be strong.[36]

In short, Nursi calls for a community founded on service to faith in pursuit of divine pleasure rather than material gain; a community in which avoidance of politics is a core value and for which hierarchical structure is eschewed. Nursi also urges believers to work for strong communal relations in dealing with the challenges to faith and spirituality. Such a community is

33. For a nuanced discussion of *dershanes*, see Yavuz, "Nur Study Circles," 297–316.

34. Nursi, *Flashes*, 219.

35. Nursi, *Flashes*, 219.

36. Nursi, *Flashes*, 219

well-suited to committing itself to positive action and nonviolence, which Nursi expects unconditionally. In the next chapter, Nursi is put into conversation with leading figures of the nonviolent struggle: Gandhi, King, and Mandela.

Chapter 8

Nursi in Conversation with Gandhi, King, and Mandela

WE BEGAN THIS ACCOUNT of Nursi's ethic and methodology by asserting that Nursi (1877–1960) belongs in the company of Mohandas Gandhi (1869–1948), Nelson Mandela (1918–2013) and Martin Luther King Jr. (1929–68). In this chapter, we shall put Nursi into conversation with these three charismatic proponents of methodologies of nonviolent societal transformation. Of these three, Gandhi was Nursi's nearest contemporary. We shall, therefore, begin with him.

Gandhi

Gandhi is renowned for his advocacy of nonviolent action as a form of civil disobedience during the movement to free India from British rule. His philosophy, from which came this strategy, had at its core the twin principles of *ahimsa* and *satyagraha*, supplemented by trust in God, self-sacrifice, transparency, and optimism.

Ahimsa

Discipleship with a great Jain teacher led Gandhi to embrace the principle of *ahimsa* ("non-harming"), the radical avoidance of harm to sentient beings in any form. This he coupled with the notion of *satyagraha* (literally, "truth-force"); as embraced by Gandhi, best understood as "the power that comes from holding fast to truth." Together, these two principles were foundational to his methodology of nonviolent civil disobedience. "If we learn the use of the weapon of *satyagraha*," Gandhi asserted, "we can employ it to overcome all hardships originating from injustice."[1] Gandhi's *satyagraha* required determination and perseverance. He thus expected followers of this method to take six vows: "truth, nonviolence, celibacy, control of the palate, nonstealing, and nonpossession."[2]

But, beyond fulfilling vows of avoidance, Gandhi's *satyagraha* involved positive action, as in his advocacy of *khadi* (homespun cloth) as a means of resistance to British rule. Indians of every social standing were urged to spin their own cotton thread for weaving into cloth locally, thus obviating the need to purchase British—or any other foreign—fabric. Gandhi himself would work long hours at spinning, which he treated as a sacred duty and spiritual experience, an expression of "passionate devotion to God."[3]

The most well-known example of positive, nonviolent action on Gandhi's part was the Salt March. According to the Salt Act imposed by the British Raj, Indians were not allowed to collect or sell salt; rather, they were required to purchase "British" salt encumbered by a steep tax—which, as sales tax always does, affected the poor disproportionately. Asserting that "there are occasions in the lifetime of a citizen when it becomes his painful duty to disobey laws,"[4] Gandhi and an expanding number of followers walked the 241 miles from his ashram in Ahmedabad to the coastal city of Dandi from March 12 to April 5, 1930. On the morning of April 6, with thousands of his followers, he waded into the sea and symbolically harvested a lump of salt, thus disobeying British law.[5] The incident led to arrest and imprisonment, of course. Thus, the Salt March became a turning point in the struggle for India's independence.

Gandhi's *satyagraha* included efforts to improve the situation of the untouchables, a categorization called by Gandhi "a blot on Hindu religion" and a dreadful "sin." In order to change society's mind-set about untouchables, Gandhi coined the name Harijan for them, which means "the children of God." He encouraged all people who were part of his movement to work for the "eradication of the evil of untouchability."[6] Poverty and

1. Wolpert, *Gandhi's Passion*, 73.
2. Wolpert, *Gandhi's Passion*, 73.
3. Wolpert, *Gandhi's Passion*, 73.
4. Wolpert, *Gandhi's Passion*, 172.
5. Wolpert, *Gandhi's Passion*, 148.
6. Wolpert, *Gandhi's Passion*, 85.

injustice are one of the two major root causes of violence. Gandhi believed that without eliminating these causes, it would be impossible to form a harmonious and peaceful community.

Addressing the untouchability question, Gandhi wrote the following:

> Socially they are lepers. Economically they are worse than slaves. Religiously they are denied entrance to places we miscall "houses of God." They are denied the use . . . of public roads, public schools, public hospitals, public wells, public taps . . . Caste Hindu lawyers and doctors will not serve them . . . They are too downtrodden to rise in revolt . . . Every Hindu should have in his home a Harijan who would be for all practical purposes a member of the family.[7]

In order to make a change in the situation of the untouchables, Gandhi began with himself. He admitted a Harijan family into his own *ashram* (or "hermitage"). We are told that Gandhi's wife was so upset by this decision that she threatened to leave him. However, Gandhi was determined that his family be an example for his followers to embrace the untouchables. Of this decision, he would later say, "The step is momentous because it so links me with the suppressed classes mission that I might have at no distant time to carry out the idea of shifting to some *Dhed* [untouchable] quarters and sharing their life . . . It is of importance to me because it enables me to demonstrate the efficacy of passive resistance in social questions and when I take the final step, it will embrace *swaraj* [freedom]."[8]

Gandhi had a dream that a Harijan would one day be elected president of India. In fact, his dream came true only fifty years after independence with the election of Dalit candidate K. R. Narayanan in 1997.[9]

Finally, Gandhi sought to seed harmony between people in religiously diverse India. Part of his *satragyaha* was fasting in order to end religious conflicts among the religious communities. Building a religiously harmonious India was one of his biggest dreams. In his activism, he worked for peace and harmony among Muslims, Hindus, and Sikhs in India.

There was an interfaith cooperation in his work. Gandhi was hailed during his time in Johannesburg as "King of the Hindus and Muslims."[10] For his activism, he held many of his meetings on the floor of a mosque in

7. Wolpert, *Gandhi's Passion*, 169.

8. Wolpert, *Gandhi's Passion*, 85.

9. Wolpert, *Gandhi's Passion*, 87.

10. Wolpert, *Gandhi's Passion*, 72.

Johannesburg, addressing both Muslims and Hindus.[11] Sadly, he was assassinated by a Hindu extremist who would say that he killed Gandhi because of "his constant and consistent pandering to the Muslims."[12]

Nursi and Gandhi Compared

While Nursi strove for freedom of religion and access to spiritual resources, Gandhi's primary concern was Indian independence. Each figure furthered his cause through employment of nonviolent civil disobedience. The method of each rested on a comprehensive principle informed by scriptures and deep faith. Nursi's was positive action (*müsbet hareket*), while for Gandhi it was *satragyaha*.

Both Nursi and Gandhi embodied their message in their lives, which touched the hearts of so many people. When it comes to sacrifice and suffering for their causes, they were at the forefront. Neither used their prestigious status as a means for worldly benefits. On the contrary, both preferred a simple life. Both quite evidently espoused the maxim that "a society is judged based on the way its most vulnerable are treated." They both struggled to establish themselves in a just society.

Both Nursi and Gandhi lived in religiously diverse societies. Gandhi wanted to unite Muslims, Hindus, and Sikhs around his cause. One of the most painful things for him was the religious conflict among these faith communities. Gandhi advocated interfaith cooperation for a just India. He would undertake extended fasts in his effort to bring interreligious conflict to an end. Nursi encouraged Christians and Muslims to set their differences aside and work together against modern challenges to faith and spirituality. Though he did not compromise on the integrity of Muslim faith and was deeply orthodox, he nevertheless sought to build alliances with others out of this deep-rootedness. As a consequence of their beliefs and efforts, both Nursi and Gandhi spent significant time in prison. Both hallowed the experience—Nursi by dubbing prison "the School of Joseph;" Gandhi by calling his cell a *mandir* ("temple").[13]

11. Wolpert, *Gandhi's Passion*, 67.
12. Wolpert, *Gandhi's Passion*, 259.
13. Wolpert, *Gandhi's Passion*, 153.

Martin Luther King Jr.

In the context of Martin Luther King Jr., racial and economic injustices were epitomized in various forms of segregation in the United States. During his inauguration as governor of Alabama in 1963, George Wallace pledged this: "segregation now, segregation tomorrow, segregation forever."[14] Alabama was in the spotlight during the civil rights movement, having become the state embodying racial injustices more than any other place. King and his supporters faced imprisonment and persecution because of their activities. King nevertheless channeled imprisonment and pressure from the governmental officials in a way that served his cause of justice. In this regard, King's Christian faith played a vital role in his fight. King was a Baptist clergyman, an eloquent preacher, and a learned theologian who frequently employed Biblical passages in his writings and sermons on civil rights matters. While in prison, King would hold religious service with his fellow prisoners. During the sit-in demonstrations, hymns would be sung. In fact, churches themselves played a crucial role in the American civil rights struggle of the 1960s. The leadership of the civil rights movement would often meet in Christian places of worship to conduct their strategic planning.[15]

King composed his most powerful writings in jail and exile. His *Letter from a Birmingham Jail* (April 16, 1963) became the symbol of his struggle. Ostensibly, King's letter was a response to Christian clergymen who had published a statement in a local newspaper chastising King for upsetting the social order in Birmingham as an "outside agitator."[16] That statement had also criticized the demonstrations led by King and called the participants "extremists."[17] In his letter, King responds to their criticism. What is remarkable about the letter is that its tone, while firm, is not angry.

Another notable aspect of the *Letter from a Birmingham Jail* is that, not only does King respond to his detractors, but he lays out a specific strategy for nonviolent resistance. He writes, "In any nonviolent campaign there are four basic steps: collection of the facts to determine whether injustices exist; negotiation; self-purification; and direct action." He then elaborates on the nature of and necessity for direct action, insisting that opportunities

14. Carson, *Autobiography of Martin Luther*, 173.

15. Carson, *Autobiography of Martin Luther*, 177.

16. Carson, *Autobiography of Martin Luther*, 189.

17. Carson, *Autobiography of Martin Luther*, 187–88.

for negotiation can be realized only if provoked: "Nonviolent direct action seeks to create such a crisis and foster such a tension that a community which has constantly refused to negotiate is forced to confront the issue. It seeks so to dramatize the issue that it can no longer be ignored." His *Letter from a Birmingham Jail* contains an assertion that remains a universal mantra for civil rights activists: "Injustice anywhere is a threat to justice everywhere."[18]

King defended his cause in Birmingham by drawing upon examples from Christian tradition:

> Just as the Prophets of the eighth century B.C. left their villages and carried their "thus saith the Lord" far beyond the boundaries of their hometowns, and just as the Apostle Paul left his village of Tarsus and carried the gospel of Jesus Christ to the far corners of the Greco-Roman world, so am I compelled to carry the gospel of freedom beyond my own hometown. Like Paul, I must constantly respond to the Macedonian call for aid.[19]

Like the apostle Paul, King was also charged with breaking the law, both by the governmental officials and by some of his fellow religious leaders. King points out that he "would be the first to advocate obeying just laws." Yet, he also maintains "one has a moral responsibility to disobey unjust laws." He concurred with Saint Augustine, who had declared, "an unjust law is no law at all"[20]—a contention King elaborates with specific examples. As King explains, "a law is unjust if it is inflicted on a minority that, as a result of being denied the right to vote, had no part in enacting or devising the law."[21] In addition, a law might be just in theory, but might be unjust in practice.[22]

Nonviolence was at the center of King's work. During his years at the Crozer Theological Seminary, King had been able to study Mahatma Gandhi's teachings on nonviolent resistance, founded on the concept of *satyagraha* ("truth-force"). Having perceived great resonance between Gandhi's *satyagraha* and Jesus' teachings on love, King asserted that "Gandhi was probably the first person in history to lift the love ethic of Jesus above mere interaction between individuals to a powerful and effective social force on

18. Carson, *Autobiography of Martin Luther*, 189.
19. Carson, *Autobiography of Martin Luther*, 189.
20. Carson, *Autobiography of Martin Luther*, 193.
21. Carson, *Autobiography of Martin Luther*, 194.
22. Carson, *Autobiography of Martin Luther*, 194.

a large scale."[23] As taught by Gandhi, unconditional love and nonviolence turned out to be "the method for social reform" that King was looking for.

Finally, many in the African American community found King and his method to be soft.[24] However, King's method of nonviolent resistance based on love came to be the most effective method in dealing with racial injustice in the United States.

King and Nursi Compared

As shown, while King was concerned with "racial and economic injustices in America," Nursi was concerned with the faith and spirituality of Muslims in Turkey. With the rise of aggressive secularism in the new republic, the institutions providing spirituality were eliminated and scientific materialism became the exclusive guide for political reforms. "Freedom from religion" became the mantra of the new state in practice. In this context, Nursi worked for freedom of religion and strove to provide spirituality. For him, faith was both a goal and a means.

Despite persecution and imprisonment, both King and Nursi made nonviolence the core principle of their resistance. Nursi maintained that, on his difficult journey, violence and conflict were not options. Otherwise, their cause would likely harm innocents. In addition, in the long run, a cause that entailed violence would eventually fail. On the premise of the qur'anic verses, Nursi makes compassion and positive action the heart of his *jihad*.

Because of their nonviolent civil disobedience, both Nursi and King were imprisoned. They were nonetheless able to transform many hearts and minds, as well as compose writings in prison. Nursi composed his most powerful writings in jail and exile, and King is no different in this regard. His *Letter from a Birmingham Jail* (April 16, 1963) became the symbol of his struggle. Instead of condemning those who were against them, both Nursi and King kept the focus on the cause at hand.

Where King relies on the Bible and the examples of the church fathers, Nursi draws on the Qur'an and the *sunna* of Muhammad. Similarly to King, Nursi was not only concerned with spiritual problems of his local community, but also that of the wider community beyond. In fact, he wanted to offer solutions to global challenges facing believers. It is not surprising,

23. Carson, *Autobiography of Martin Luther*, 24.

24. Carson, *Autobiography of Martin Luther*, 266.

therefore, that even people of other faiths have been drawn to Nursi's writings and are able to relate to them.

In their civil disobedience, both Nursi and King recognized the difference between "just and unjust laws."[25] Facing persecution because of his writings and activities for providing spirituality, Nursi asked the government to at least apply the principles of secularism to his case. He pointed out that what is generally understood from secularism is the separation of state and religion. In this sense, just as religion should not dictate to the state, neither should the state promote atheism. Thus, as Nursi saw it, government's prohibition—in the name of secularism—of the freedom to practice religion was unjust. Hence, he refused to conform to edicts such as those pertaining to wearing brimless hats and continued practice of his religion according to the prophetic example as much as he could. He was charged with breaking the law—a law that he himself saw as unjust.

Significantly, the methodologies of both Nursi and King were criticized for their softness. Among Nursi's critics were Muslims who indeed shared his goals and who might even admit that study of the *Risale* could lead to societal transformation in the long run; nevertheless they wanted change at a faster rate. Nursi's followers insist that, though painstaking, his was still the more efficient method, in that it avoided harm to civilians. In the course of time, Nursi's method of reading the *Risale* both individually and collectively has indeed been able to form faithful minds and hearts.

Nelson Mandela

Nelson Mandela was born in 1918. From the early years of his life, dismantling the injustices of apartheid in South Africa became his cause. While the symptoms of apartheid began to take form under the Dutch Empire in the eighteenth century, it was institutionalized and fully embraced in the form of segregation and discrimination in 1948 when the National Party came to power.

In his autobiography, *Long Walk to Freedom*, Mandela writes about his involvement in the struggle to end apartheid as follows: "I cannot pinpoint a moment when I became politicized, when I knew that I would spend my life in the liberation struggle. To be an African in South Africa means that one is politicized from the moment of one's birth, whether one acknowledges or

25. Carson, *Autobiography of Martin Luther*, 193.

not."[26] Mandela then describes the situation of an African in South Africa: "When he grows up, he can hold African Only jobs, rent a house in Africans Only townships, ride Africans Only trains, and be stopped at any time of the day or night and be ordered to produce a pass, failing which he will be arrested and thrown in jail. His life is circumscribed by racist laws and regulations that cripple his growth, dim his potential, and stunt his life. This was the reality."[27] For Mandela, one would not need to have an "epiphany" or a "moment of truth" in order to be part of the struggle. The indignities and injustices done to his people through the apartheid system did not give any chance but a desire to fight the unjust system.[28]

Yet his activities did not come without a major cost. Mandela was demonized as a terrorist, tortured, and imprisoned for twenty-seven years. He suffered not only under the severe conditions of prison, but separation from his family and loved ones. In fact, the death of his mother and eldest son coincided with his time in prison. He could not attend their funerals because state officials did not allow him to say his farewell. Mandela was released from the prison in 1990 when he was seventy-one. In 1994, he was elected as the first black president in South Africa's first multiracial election. We should remember that it was only the White Afrikaners who were allowed to vote.

In the face of injustice, discrimination, and persecution, Mandela never lost hope. He deeply trusted in the goodness of his fellow human beings. Mandela believed that change would eventually overcome:

> I never lost hope that this great transformation [the end to apartheid] would occur. Not only because of the great heroes I have already cited, but because of the courage of the ordinary men and women of my country. I always knew that deep down in every human heart, there is mercy and generosity. No one is born hating another person because of the color of his skin, or his background, or his religion. People must learn to hate, and if they can learn to hate, they can be taught to love, for love comes more naturally to the human heart than its opposite. Even in the grimmest times in prison, when my comrades and I were pushed to our limits, I would see a glimmer of humanity in one of the guards, perhaps just for a second, but it was enough to reassure me and keep me

26. Mandela, *Long Walk to Freedom*, 95.
27. Mandela, *Long Walk to Freedom*, 95.
28. Mandela, *Long Walk to Freedom*, 95.

going. Man's goodness is a flame that can be hidden but never extinguished.[29]

As seen in the case of Nursi, Mandela would also be able to see positive aspects in evil. While Nursi would regard the injustice he and his students faced as part of the divine plan, for Mandela the evil in the form of apartheid served to bring the best out of people. The injustices of the apartheid system produced exemplary figures fighting to end evil; among them are the Oliver Tambos, the Walter Sisilus, the Chief Luthulis, the Yusuf Dadoos, the Bram Fischers, and the Robert Sobukwes. Mandela points out that "perhaps it requires such depth of oppression to create such heights of character."[30]

Nursi and Mandela Compared

Nursi spent more than thirty years in prison or exile; Nelson Mandela, twenty-seven years of continuous incarceration. When Mandela emerged from the long period of imprisonment as the most powerful man in South Africa, the most remarkable thing about him was his eagerness for forgiveness and reconciliation with his enemies. His philosophy for this next stage of his life is encapsulated in these words: "As I walked out the door toward the gate that would lead to my freedom, I knew if I didn't leave my bitterness and hatred behind, I'd still be in prison."

Mandela celebrated his freedom from prison by engaging positively with his former oppressors. He visited the widow of Hendrik Verwoerd, the former prime minister known for his policies of the apartheid. He unconditionally forgave the state prosecutor, Percy Yutar, who had demanded a life sentence for him, saying that Yutar had only been doing his job. When Mandela was elected president of South Africa, he invited two of his warders in prison to attend his inauguration. Thus he demonstrated his belief in "the essential humanity of even those who had kept him behind bars," his certainty that "forgiveness liberates the soul, it removes fear."

Similarly, when, in the mid-fifties, after more than thirty years of imprisonment and exile, he and his writings were acquitted of all the charges,

---

29. Mandela, *Long Walk to Freedom*, 622.
30. Mandela, *Long Walk to Freedom*, 622.

Nursi was a highly influential man. Yet, the focus of his last lesson to his students was forgiveness of his oppressors.[31]

Elsewhere in his writings, Nursi also urges his students to forgive their oppressors. By way of illustration, he refers to a time when, from a prison window, he caught sight of a girl who turned out to be the daughter of the prosecutor who convicted him. For the sake of this man's daughter, Nursi gave up wishing any ill to befall him.

As happened with Mandela, some of Nursi's statements on reconciliation and forgiveness have become mantras for his students:

We are competitors of love; we do not have time for enmity.

The guiding principle of our community is to love love and to hate hatred.

If you really want to hate something, hate the hatred in your heart.

Nursi Among the Champions of Nonviolence

In his approach to transformation of society, Nursi has much in common with Gandhi, King, and Mandela. Where Gandhi fought for Indian independence, where Mandela and King fought for racial and economic justice, Nursi strove incessantly for the freedom to practice faith and for access to spiritual resources for all people. Thus, writing and reading would become for him and his followers the most potent means of creative, nonviolent civil disobedience; the production of literature focusing on spirituality would become a compelling agent of change. Where Gandhi's legacy is emblemized by the Salt March, Mandela's by his election to presidency, and King's by his *Letter from a Birmingham Jail* and speeches like *I Have a Dream*, Nursi's resides in his magnum opus, the *Risale*, and the community that nurtured its formation, disseminated it, and embodies its teachings in the present. That community continues *jihad* as he understood and taught it: striving on the Godward path via positive action (*müsbet hareket*).

---

31. For the letter in Turkish, see Nursi, *Emirdağ Lahikası II*, 630–38.

Conclusion

WE HAVE BEGUN WITH the thesis that Nursi's positive action (*müsbet hareket*) and his nonviolent *jihad* of civil disobedience defied some suppositions about Islam and Muslims, that Islam is an inherently violent religion; that it is a political ideology; and that it is unable to accommodate secularism.

As we have explained, for early twentieth-century Turkey's pious Muslims, imposition of secularism from the top down was a painful experience. Whereas in the United States, secularism and the separation of the church and state came as a means of promoting more religious freedom, in the case of Turkey, it occurred as "freedom from religion." Institutions providing Islamic education and spirituality were shut down. The new Turkish state embarked on a journey of promoting scientific materialism and positivism. There was almost no room for Islamic values and culture, no freedom of assembly for religious reasons.

Considering that, in the post-Ottoman Turkish society, religion was still one of the most important phenomena, the New Republic's approach of religion created a major spiritual gap. Within this space, Nursi offered resources in order to answer the Muslim community's questions concerning faith and spirituality: his Qur'an commentary, the *Risale-i Nur*, provided a map for believers in the new context. The methods he taught—positive action (*müsbet hareket*) and nonviolent *jihad* of civil disobedience—became the hallmarks of the community that formed around his writings: the Nur Community.

Nursi's philosophy is best summarized in his last lesson to his students,[1] in which he provides guidelines and principles for believers to cultivate his approach based on the Qur'an and prophetic example. Let us

---

1. For the full transcript of this lesson in English, see Nursi, *Emirdağ Letters*, 506–12.

close by summarizing its core tenets, all of which have application in the present day.

The cultivation of positive action and nonviolence should begin from the heart and mind, he emphasizes, because construction of a peaceful society can begin only after hearts and minds are at peace and fully liberated. Even in the most desperate situation, he reminds us that there is something beautiful to see and appreciate in the universe. He offers this motto: "the one who sees beautifully thinks beautifully; thinking of what is good makes life pleasant."[2] Thus Nursi was able to see positive aspects, even of his exile and imprisonment.

Impotence (*acz*), poverty (*fakr*), compassion (*şefkat*), and contemplation (*tefekkür*) are the most important elements of Nursi's inward *jihad*. Believers should always be aware of their weakness and need in relation to God. In addition, they should carry compassion for the entire creation and contemplate God's universe with awe and admiration.

Nursi believed that the time of physical *jihad* was over. He believed that faith is best served through spiritual *jihad*; by "*jihad* of word" rather than "*jihad* of sword." Even within the most difficult conditions, believers should never stoop to violence and conflict, because they cost the lives of innocent people.

Nursi attempted to revive the spiritual meaning of martyrdom. With renewed emphasis on the prophetic *hadith* that "the ink of scholars will outweigh the blood of the martyrs on the scales," he insisted that living up to the teachings of the Qur'an and prophetic example, doing service to faith, and studying his *Risale* could earn the same reward as laying down one's body in armed defense of one's religion.

In Nursi's time, the vast majority of the Muslim world was still ruled under colonialism. Even within those conditions, Nursi insisted that the enemies of the community of believers were not external; they lay within. As he saw it, the major enemies of the Muslim community were ignorance, poverty, and disunity. To deal with these threats he offered education, material progress, and unity.

For Nursi, people of other faiths need not be seen as threats to Muslims. Rather, he regarded them as allies in the struggle against challenges to faith in the new age. He remarked that pious Christian missionaries and Muslims should leave their theological differences aside and work together on those common challenges.

2. Nursi, *Mektubat*, 669.

The modern believer's service of faith should be for the sake of God, never for worldly or personal benefits. Such service should be provided for free. Nursi himself lived a frugal life, not even accepting gifts, thus setting a high standard for this approach.

Nursi advised his students to avoid politics as much as possible. Thus his assertion, "I seek refuge in God from politics and Satan," became an important motto for his students. For Nursi, service to faith through politics is an impossibility because, instead of adhering to the prophetic principle "Power is in right; right is not in power,"[3] politics too often follows the watchwords "Might is right" or "All power to the strongest."[4]

In the face of excessive individualism in secular societies, Nursi emphasized community. He believed that the challenges of the new age could only be tackled as a group. He strongly encouraged his followers to read his *Risale* communally in places called *dershanes*. However, Nursi believed that the community of believers should not be hierarchical. He often turned away those who wanted to visit him. He did not even want his grave to be known by his followers. He always referred his followers to the text of the *Risale*. In this sense, he believed in "the priesthood of all believers," to borrow a popular term from Protestant thought.

In his approach of transforming society, Nursi stands in the company of Gandhi, Mandela, and Dr. King—for all of whom nonviolence, compassion, and reconciliation were in the center of their *jihad* to bring justice to their society.

3. Nursi, *Words*, 563.

4. Nursi, *Words*, 563.

Appendix

A Portion from *Nursi's Last Teaching to the Students of the Risale-i Nur before His Death.*[1]

My Dear Brothers!

Our duty is to act positively; it is not to act negatively. It is solely to serve the cause of belief in accordance with divine pleasure and not interfere with God's concerns. We are charged with responding with patience and thanks to every difficulty we may meet in the positive service of belief, a consequence of which is the preservation of public order and security.

Taking myself as an example, I say this: Formerly I never bowed before tyranny or humiliating treatment. Numerous events established that I could never endure to be treated in that way. For example, not rising to my feet before the Commander-in-Chief in Russia, and my giving no importance to the pashas' questions in the Military Court even when under threat of execution, as well as my attitude to four commanders, all show that I never bowed before domination. But these last thirty years, for the sake of acting positively and not acting negatively and not interfering in God's concerns, I have responded with patience and resignation to all the treatment I have received. I have met it with patience and resignation like Jarjis (upon whom be peace) and those who suffered the extreme difficulties of the Battles of Badr and Uhud.

Yes, for example, I did not even curse a Public Prosecutor whose eighty-one errors I had proved in court, as a result of whose false accusations the decision was taken against us. For the essential matter at this time is *jihad* of the word or moral *jihad* (*cihad-ı mânevî*). It is to form a barrier

1. For the full letter, see Nursi, *Emirdağ Letters*, 506–12.

against moral and spiritual destruction, and to assist internal order and security with all our strength.

Yes, there is a power in our way, but this force is for preserving public order. According to the principle of *"No bearer of burdens can bear the burden of another"* (Q 6:164, etc.), the brother, family, or children of a criminal cannot be held responsible for him. Because of this, throughout my life I have endeavored with all my strength to maintain public order. This force may not be employed internally, but only against external aggression. Our duty in accordance with the above verse is to assist the maintenance of internal order and security with all our strength. It is for this reason that within the world of Islam internal actions disturbing public order have been only one in a thousand, and they arose from differences in interpretation of the law. The most important condition of the *jihad* of the word is not interfering in God's concerns; that is: "Our duty is to serve; its results are Almighty God's concern. We are charged with carrying out our duty, and are obliged to do so."

Like Jalaluddin Kharzamshah, I have learnt from the Qur'an to say: "My duty is to serve religious belief; it is Almighty God's concern to give success or not to give it," and to act with sincerity.

External aggression may be met with force, for the enemy's possessions and dependents are like booty. But this is not the case internally. Internal action has to be action which accords with the true meaning of sincerity in positive, non-physical (*mânevî*) fashion against the moral and spiritual (*mânevî*) destruction. External and internal *jihad* are completely different. Almighty God has now given me millions of true students, but internally we shall act positively only to maintain public order and security. The difference at this time between internal and external non-physical *jihad* is truly great . . .

My brothers! My illness is very severe. Perhaps I shall die soon or be prevented from speaking altogether, as I am sometimes now. Therefore, saying they are the lesser of two evils, my Nur brothers of the hereafter should not attack certain unfortunate erring people because of their mistakes. They should always act positively. Acting negatively is not our concern. For action internally may not be negative. Since some of the politicians cause no harm to the *Risale-i Nur* and are a little tolerant, look on them as the lesser of two evils. Cause them no harm and do them good so that you may be saved from a greater evil.

Also, internal non-physical *jihad* is to work against the moral and spiritual devastation. It is not material or physical service that is needed, but non-physical and moral service. For this reason we do not interfere with the politicians, nor have the politicians any right to busy themselves with us!

For example, I have forgiven a certain party despite its having inflicted thousands of sorts of difficulties on me, and even thirty years of imprisonment and persecution. And I have been the means of 95 percent of those unfortunates being saved from insult, criticism, and oppression. For according to the verse, *"No bearer of burdens can bear the burden of another,"* we ascribed the fault to only 5 percent. The party which opposed us has no right whatsoever to complain about us now.

In one court, even, attempts were made to convict us, seventy people, as a result of the delusions of spies and informers and to convict me due to misunderstandings and carelessness and eighty errors by attaching false meanings to certain parts of the *Risale-i Nur*—as had been proved in a number of courts. But while a prisoner, one of your brothers [Nursi]who had been subject to the worst attacks saw the Public Prosecutor's three-year-old child out of the window. He asked and they told him "It is the Public Prosecutor's daughter." For the sake of that innocent child, he did not curse the Prosecutor. Indeed, since the troubles he had inflicted had resulted in advertising the *Risale-i Nur*, that non-material miracle, and of its dissemination, they had been transformed into mercy.

My Brothers! Perhaps I shall soon die. This age has another sickness; sicknesses like egotism, self-centredness, self-advertisement, the desire to pass one's life comfortably in accordance with the fantasies of modern civilization, and to be obsessed with this. The first and most important lesson the *Risale-i Nur* has learnt from the Qur'an is the need to give up egotism, selfishness, and self-advertisement, so that the saving of belief may be served with true sincerity. Thanks be to God, numerous individuals have emerged who have gained that maximum sincerity. There are many who sacrifice their egotism, reputation, and good name for the smallest matter of belief. For example, when the enemies of one unfortunate student of the *Risale-i Nur* became friends, divine mercy made him lose his voice because their conversations with him increased. Also, the looks of people who consider him admiringly strike him like the evil eye, and cause him pain. Shaking hands even causes him distress as though he had received a blow.

He was asked: "What is this condition of yours? Since you have millions of friends, why do you not meet with them for their sake?" He replied:

"Since our way is maximum sincerity, it necessitates preferring a single, eternal matter of belief to rule over the whole world even, were it to be given, let alone egotism and selfishness. For example, in the midst of the enemy's fire in the front lines in the war, he preferred a single point of a single letter of a single verse of the All-Wise Qur'an, and ordered his scribe, Habib, when under the rain of the bullets: 'Take out the notebook!', and dictated that point to him on horseback. That is to say, he did not abandon a single letter or point of the Qur'an in the face of the enemy bullets; he preferred them to saving his own life."

—*Said Nursi*

Bibliography

Abu-Rabi', Ibrahim M., ed. *Spiritual Dimensions of Bediuzzaman Said Nursi's Risale-i Nur*. New York: State University of New York Press, 2008.

Afsaruddin, Asma. *Striving in the Path of God: Jihad and Martyrdom in Islamic Thought*. Oxford: Oxford University Press, 2013.

Akgündüz, Ahmet. *Arşiv Belgeleri Işığında Bediüzzaman Said Nursi ve İlmi Şahsiyeti, Vol. 2*. Istanbul: OSAV, 2013.

Akyol, Mustafa. *Islam Without Extremes: A Muslim Case for Liberty*. New York: Norton, 2011.

al-Ghazali, Abu Hamid. *Ihyā' 'Ulūm al-Dīn, Vol. 1*. Cairo: al-Quds, 2012.

———. *On the Boundaries of Theological Tolerance in Islam: Abu Hamid al-Ghazali's Faysal al-Tafriqa*. Translated by Sherman A. Jackson. Oxford: Oxford University Press, 2002.

al-Suyuti, Jalal al-Din. *al-Jami' al-Saghir*. Beirut: Dār al-Kutub al-'Ilmiyya, 2004.

Aslan, Reza. *No God But God: Origins, Evolution, and Future of Islam*. New York: Random House, 2006.

Becker, Ernest. *The Denial of Death*. New York: Free Press, 1997.

Berkes, Niyazi. *The Development of Secularism in Turkey*. New York: Routledge, 1968.

Blackwell, Gary E. "Return or Rereading: The Spirituality of Brian D. Mclaren." PhD diss., New Orleans Baptist Theological Seminary, 2015.

Blankinship, Khalid. *The End of the Jihad State*. New York: State University of New York Press, 1994.

Bonner, Michael. *Jihad in Islamic History: Doctrines and Practice*. Princeton: Princeton University Press, 2006.

Carson, Clayborne, ed. *The Autobiography of Martin Luther King*. New York: Warner, 1998.

Cevdet, Abdullah. "Mezheb-i Bahaullah—Din-i Ümem." *Ictihad* 144 (March 1922) 3015–17.

Dağlı, Caner. "Conquest and Conversion, War and Peace in the Qur'an." In *The Study Qur'an: A New Translation and Commentary*, edited by Seyyed Hossein Nasr and C. K. Dağlı, 1805–18. New York: HarperOne, 2015.

Demir, Ahmet Ishak. *Cumhuriyet Aydınlarının Islam'a Bakışı*. Istanbul: Ensar Neşriyat, 2004.

d'Holbach, Baron. *Good Sense or Natural Ideas Opposed to Supernatural*. New York: Wright & Owen, 1931.

el-Acluni, Isma'il b. Ahmad. *Keshfu'l-Hafa*. Edited by Ahmad al-Qalash. Cairo: Dar al-Turath, n.d.

BIBLIOGRAPHY

Ersoy, Mehmet Akif. *Safahat.* Edited by Ertuğrul Düzdağ. Ankara: Kültür Bakanlığı Yayınları, 1987.

———. *Safahat.* Edited by Ertuğrul Düzdağ. Istanbul: İz Yayıncılık, 1991.

Esposito, John. *What Everyone Needs to Know About Islam.* Oxford: Oxford University Press, 2013.

Faggioli, Massimo. *John XXIII: The Medicine of Mercy.* Collegeville, MN: Liturgical, 2014.

Findley, Carter Vaughn. *Turkey, Islam, Nationalism, and Modernity: A History, 1789–2007.* New Haven: Yale University Press, 2010.

Haleem, M. A. S. Abdel, trans. *The Qur'an: English and Parallel Arabic Text.* Oxford: Oxford University Press, 2010.

Hallaq, Wael B. *Introduction to Islamic Law.* Cambridge: Cambridge University Press, 2009.

Hanioğlu, M. Şükrü. *Atatürk: An Intellectual Biography.* Princeton: Princeton University Press, 2011.

———. "Garbcılar: Their Attitudes toward Religion and Their Impact on the Official Ideology of the Turkish Republic." *Studia Islamica* 86.2 (1997) 134–58.

Hillenbrand, Carole. *Introduction to Islam: Beliefs and Practices in Historical Perspective.* London: Thames & Hudson, 2015.

Hodgson, Marshal G. S. *The Venture of Islam: Conscience and History in a World Civilization, Vol. 3: The Gunpowder Empires and Modern Times.* Chicago: University of Chicago Press, 1977.

Kahf, Monzer. "Waqf." http://www.oxfordislamicstudies.com/article/opr/t342/e0467.

Kırkıncı, Mehmet. *Hayatım-Hatıralarım.* Istanbul: Zafer Yayınları, 2013.

Kunkel, Joseph. "The Spiritual Side of Peacemaking." In *Spiritual and Political Dimensions of Nonviolence and Peace,* edited by David Boersema and Katy Gray Brown, 31–42. Rodopi: Amsterdam, 1994.

LeBuffe, Michael. "Paul-Henri Thiry (Baron) d'Holbach." https://plato.stanford.edu/entries/holbach/#Aca.

Lewis, Bernard. *The Emergence of Modern Turkey.* London: Oxford University Press, 1968.

Lewis, C. S. *Letters to an American Lady.* Grand Rapids: Eerdmans, 1967.

Linke, Lilo. *Allah Dethroned: A Journey Through Modern Turkey.* London: Constable, 1937.

Lipka, Michael. "Why America's 'Nones' Left Religion Behind." http://www.pewresearch.org/fact-tank/2016/08/24/why-americas-nones-left-religion-behind/.

Mandela, Nelson. *Long Walk to Freedom.* New York: Little, Brown, & Co., 1994.

Mardin, Şerif. "Reflections on Said Nursi's Life and Thought." In *Islam at the Crossroads: On the Life and Thought of Bediuzzaman Said Nursi,* edited by Ibrahim M. Abu-Rabi', 45–50. Albany: State University of New York, 2003.

———. *Religion and Social Change in Modern Turkey: The Case of Bediuzzaman Said Nursi.* New York: Syracuse University Press, 1989.

Michel, Thomas F. *Said Nursi's Views on Muslim-Christian Understanding.* Istanbul: Söz Basım Yayin, 2005.

Nasr, Seyyed Hossein, et al. *The Study Qur'an: A New Translation and Commentary.* New York: HarperOne, 2015.

"Nostra Aetate." http://www.vatican.va/archive/hist_councils/ii_vatican_council/documents/vat-ii_decl_19651028_nostra-aetate_en.html.

Nursi, Abdurrahman. *Bedîüzzaman'ın Tarihçe-i Hayatı.* Istanbul: Necm-i İstikbâl Matbaası, 1919.

BIBLIOGRAPHY

Nursi, Bediuzzaman Said. *Barla Lahikası*. Istanbul: Söz Basım, 2012.

———. *The Damascus Sermon*. Translated by Şükran Vahide. Istanbul: Sözler, 1996.

———. *Emirdağ Lahikası, Vol. I*. Istanbul: Söz Basım Yayin, 2012

———. *Emirdağ Lahikasi, Vol. II*. Istanbul: Söz Basım Yayin, 2012.

———. *Emirdağ Letters*. Translated by Şükran Vahide. Istanbul: Sözler, 2016.

———. *The Flashes*. Translated by Şükran Vahide. Istanbul: Sözler, 2004.

———. "Hakikat." *Dini Ceride*. no:70. Mart 1909.

———. *Hutbe-i Şamiye in İlk Dönem Eserleri*. Istanbul: Söz Basım Yayin, 2012.

———. *Ilk Dönem Eserleri: Divan-i Harb-i Örfi*. Istanbul: Söz Basım Yayin, 2012.

———. *İşârâtül-İ'câz*. Istanbul: Söz Basım, 2012.

———. *Kastamonu Lahikası*. Istanbul: Söz Basım Yayin, 2012.

———. *Lem'alar*. Istanbul: Sözler, 2012.

———. *The Letters*. Translated by Şükran Vahide. Istanbul: Sözler, 2001.

———. *Mektubat*. Istanbul: Söz Basım Yayin, 2012.

———. *Mesnevî-i Nuriye*. Istanbul: Söz Basım Yayin, 2012.

———. "Muhakemat." In *Risale-i Nur Külliyati, Vol. 2*, 1986–2039. Istanbul: Nesil, 1996.

———. "Münazarat." In *Ilk Dönem Eserleri*, 433–525. Istanbul: Söz Basım Yayin, 2012.

———. *The Rays*. Translated by Sükran Vahide. Istanbul: Sözler, 2004.

———. *Signs of Miraculousness*. Translated by Şükran Vahide. Istanbul: Sözler, 2004.

———. *Sikke-i Tasdik-i Gaybî*. Istanbul: Söz Basım Yayin, 2012.

———. *Sözler*. Istanbul: Sözler, 2013.

———. *Şu'alar*. Istanbul: Söz Basım Yayin, 2012.

———. "Şualar." In *Risale-i Nur Külliyati, Vol. 1*, 831–1152. Istanbul: Nesil, 1996.

———. "Sunuhat." In *Ilk Dönem Eserleri*, 297–349. Istanbul: Söz Basım Yayin, 2012.

———. *Tarihçe-i Hayat*. Istanbul: RNK, 2012.

———. *Tarihçe-i Hayat*. Istanbul: Söz Basım Yayin, 2012.

———. *The Words*. Translated by Şükran Vahide. Istanbul: Sözler, 2008

Ramadan, Tariq. *Islam and the Arab Awakening*. Oxford: Oxford University Press, 2012.

Sachiko, Murata, and William C. Chittick. *The Vision of Islam*. St. Paul: Paragon, 1994.

"Sahih Muslim: Book 45, Hadith 54." http://sunnah.com/muslim/45/54.

Şahiner, Necmeddin. *Bilinmeyen Taraflarıyla Bediuzzaman Said Nursi*. Istanbul: Nesil, 2013.

———. *Haşir Risalesi Nasıl Yazıldı?* Istanbul: Zafer Yayınları, 1997.

———. *Son Şahitler: Bediuzzaman Said Nursi'yi Anlatiyor*. 6 vols. Istanbul: Nesil, 2004–7.

———. "Süleyman Hünkar Maddesi." In *Son Şahitler II*, 268–73. Istanbul: Yeni Asya, 1981.

Sayilgan, M. Salih. "The Importance of the *Sunna* in Islamic Spirituality: Said Nursi's Approach." In *The Companion to Said Nursi Studies*, edited by Ian S. Markham and Zeyneb Sayilgan, 192–204. Eugene, OR: Pickwick, 2017.

Schleifer, S. Abdullah. "*Jihad*: Modernist Apologists, Modern Apologetics." *The Islamic Quarterly* 28.1 (1984) 25–46.

Sonn, Tamara. *Islam: A Brief History*. Oxford: Wiley-Blackwell, 2010.

Steinfels, Peter. "Modernity and Belief: Charles Taylor's 'A Secular Age.'" *Commonweal*, May 5, 2008. https://www.commonwealmagazine.org/modernity-belief.

Taylor, Charles. *A Secular Age*. Cambridge: Belknap, 2007.

Turner, Colin. *The Qur'an Revealed: A Critical Analysis of Said Nursi's Epistle of Light*. Berlin: Gerlach, 2013.

Turner, Colin, and Hasan Horkuc. *Makers of Islamic Civilization: Said Nursi.* London: Tauris, 2009.

Vahide, Şükran. *The Author of the Risale-i Nur Collection: Bediuzzaman Said Nursi.* Istanbul: Sözler, 2004.

———. *Biography of Bediuzzaman Said Nursi: the Author of the Risale-i Nur.* Istanbul: Sözler, 1992.

———. *Islam in Modern Turkey: An Intellectual Biography of Bediuzzaman Said Nursi.* New York: Syracuse University Press, 2005.

———. "The Life and Times of Bediuzzaman Said Nursi." *The Muslim World* 89.3–4 (1999) 208–44.

———. "Said Nursi from the Ottoman to the Republic Periods: A Short Biography." In *The Companion to Said Nursi Studies,* edited by Ian S. Markham and Zeyneb Sayilgan, 23–40. Eugene, OR: Pickwick, 2017.

Vanderhaar, Gerard A. *Active Nonviolence: A Way of Personal Peace.* Eugene, OR: Wipf & Stock, 2013.

Wolpert, Stanley. *Gandhi's Passion: The Life and Legacy of Mahatma Gandhi.* Oxford: Oxford University Press, 2001.

Yavuz, M. Hakan. "Nur Study Circles (*Dershanes*) and the Formation of New Religious Consciousness in Turkey." In *Islam at the Crossroads: On the Life and Thought of Bediuzzaman Said Nursi,* edited by Ibrahim M Abu-Rabi', 297–316. Albany: State University of New York Press, 2003.

Yazır, Elmalılı Hamdi. *Hak Dini Kur'an Dili.* 6 vols. Istanbul: Eser, 1979.

Zürcher, Erik J. *The Young Turk Legacy and Nation Building: From the Ottoman Empire to Ataturk's Turkey.* London: Tauris, 2010.